# THE HEALTHY
# **FOOD**
# DIRECTORY

# THE HEALTHY
# **FOOD**
# DIRECTORY

## MICHAEL VAN STRATEN

## NEW MILLENNIUM BOOKS
Vancouver

First published in Canada in 1999 by
NEW MILLENNIUM BOOKS
8036 Enterprise Street, Burnaby
British Columbia V5A 1V7
Tel: (604) 415-2444  Fax: (604) 415-3444

ISBN 1-894067-11-8

*Note from the publisher*
Information given in this book is not intended to be
taken as a replacement for medical advice. Any person
with a condition requiring medical attention should
consult a qualified medical practitioner or therapist.

This book was conceived, designed,
and produced by
THE IVY PRESS LIMITED
2/3 St. Andrews Place
Lewes, East Sussex BN7 1UP

Art Director: CLARE BARBER
Designer: JANE LANAWAY
Editorial Director: SOPHIE COLLINS
Managing Editor: ANNE TOWNLEY
Text Editor: MANDY GREENFIELD
DTP Designer: CHRIS LANAWAY
Studio Photography: IAN PARSONS, GUY RYECART,
WALTER GARDINER
Illustrations: MADELEINE HARDY

Reproduction and printing in China by
Hong Kong Graphics and Printing Ltd.

The publishers are grateful to Holt Studios
Photograph Library for permission to reproduce
photographs on pp. 24l and 103r.

# CONTENTS

HAZELNUTS

## INTRODUCTION
## What is a Healthy Diet?

*What we need from any healthy diet is energy, which is obtained by consuming a mixture of foods providing protein, fats, carbohydrates, vitamins, and minerals. The wider the variety of foods that we eat, the less likely we are to be deficient in any of the essential nutrients that our bodies need.*

REDCURRANTS

*Long before the supermarket, freezer, microwave, and food processor, humans were hunter-gatherers living largely on nuts, berries, fruit, and roots. We gradually added meat, dairy products, cereals, and vegetables to our diet. Humans thus became omnivores and on this mixed diet survived and developed through the millennia. We did not know about vitamins, minerals, and proteins, yet we thrived and prospered. Why, then, is everyone now obsessed with the topic of nutrition? At the end of the twentieth*

VENISON

century Western society is reaping a bitter harvest from the diseases of civilization: heart disease, high blood pressure, cancer, obesity, gallstones, liver failure, and kidney problems are diseases of overconsumption.

The food we eat has changed more during the past 100 years than in the previous 100,000 and we have been slow to adapt to these changes, most of which have not been for the better. High-fat, high-salt, high-sugar products, storage, processing, intensive farming, growth hormones and antibiotics have not added to the nutritional value of what we eat today. But we are nothing if not inventive, and the tide is beginning to turn. There is a growing interest in better ways of eating. Health-food stores, ethnic and vegetarian restaurants, and organic farms are booming, and we can all benefit.

PAPAYA

ASPARAGUS

# The Mediterranean Diet

Why is it that in almost all the countries bordering the Mediterranean, people are healthier than those in northern Europe, Britain, and the United States? The reason is the Mediterranean diet: a diet that results in less heart disease, fewer strokes, and a much lower incidence of a number of different cancers. How can this be possible when you have seen Mediterraneans smoking, feasting on *pâté de foie gras*, salami, smelly cheese, and vast quantities of wine?

There are two reasons. First, Mediterraneans consume enormous quantities of fruit, vegetables, and salads, which are rich in the protective antioxidants. Second, their diet has been far less influenced by the march of modern food technology, and they eat far less of the highly processed, high-fat, high-sugar foods: olive oil instead of butter and animal or hydrogenated vegetable fats for cooking; masses of garlic, which is both heart-protective and has anti-cancer properties; far more fish and seafood; and much smaller quantities of red meat.

COLORFUL MEDITERRANEAN FOODS

Antioxidants act as scavengers, cleansing the system of harmful free radicals and protecting against their destructive power. Olive oil in particular is lavishly supplied with vitamin E, one of the most powerful antioxidants, and scientific research now supports the view of olive oil as a protective food-medicine, as long held in peasant lore throughout the Mediterranean. This antioxidant value would be enough in itself to account for the protective effect on the heart of the Mediterranean diet, but two recent studies have also shown that, on diets rich in olive oil, volunteers showed marked reductions in their blood cholesterol.

Not for nothing do Cretan peasants quite often breakfast on a chunk of bread accompanied by half a tumbler of olive oil.

## SUPER FOOD

● The Mediterranean diet is full of wonderful dishes, many of which are prepared without meat—wonderful pasta served with vegetables or seafood; imaginative salads; dishes made with peppers, eggplants, and olives; simply broiled or baked fish; rice dishes containing everything but the kitchen sink; low-fat goat's and sheep's cheeses; and the delights of coarse country bread with an olive oil and garlic dip to replace high-fat butter.

# Vegetarianism

PROTEIN FOODS FOR VEGETARIANS

If you are going to be a vegetarian, it is vital that you learn to do it properly. There are endless old wives' tales about the evils that will follow if you don't eat lots of meat. None of them is true, though they are often trotted out by doctors, mothers-in-law, and grannies. You will not become weak if you stop eating meat, nor will you become impotent if you are a man, infertile if you are a woman or stupid. Billions of people throughout the world are healthy, strong, virile, fertile, intelligent, and active vegetarians.

Just because you remove meat, fish, and poultry from your daily meals does not mean there is a reason to worry about your health; in fact, it is likely to be a great deal better without the intake of saturated animal fats. Vegetarians experience less heart disease, less high blood pressure, and less cancer of the stomach and bowel than meat-eaters. Vitamins D and $B_{12}$ are the only nutrients that may possibly be lacking (see *Macrobiotic Diet on p. 10*), but this is easily overcome (see *Vitamins on pp. 216–17*).

Vegetarian children and teenagers need a high-energy diet. Make sure that they have plenty of high-energy foods and not too much of the very bulky foods, which may fill them up but leave them short of calories. Dairy products, nuts, seeds, fats, and oils provide more calories and less bulk. For this reason bringing up children on a totally vegan diet (that is, without eggs or any dairy products) can be difficult and I certainly do not recommend it.

Protein has always been the vexed question of vegetarianism. But as long as your daily diet contains a mixture of vegetable protein sources—cereals and legumes, dairy products, eggs, nuts, seeds, fruit, and vegetables—it will provide you with all the protein you need.

## AN IRON CONSTITUTION

● Most doctors seem to worry about their vegetarian patients becoming anemic, because everyone associates the provision of iron with meat and liver. There is plenty of iron in wholewheat bread, good cereals, and dark-green leafy vegetables, which the careful vegetarian will be eating in abundance. Since the absorption of iron is greatly improved in the presence of vitamin C—and again the good vegetarian will generally be consuming much more fresh fruit than the average meat-eater—anemia is rarely a problem for vegetarians.

9

# Macrobiotic Diet

YIN AND YANG FOODS

Early in the twentieth century George Ohsawa, an American Japanese living in California, applied the philosophy of Zen to nutrition. He constructed a diet of the most "balanced" foods, based on the yin/yang principle and working through seven stages to the optimum seventh level, which was to be brown rice only—his definition of the perfect food. For the beginner, a period of gradually giving up all meat preceded level one, which comprised 40 percent cereals, 30 percent vegetables, 10 percent soup, and 20 percent animal foods (excluding meat). By level three the proportions were 60:30:10, now excluding animal protein. Level seven, the brown rice diet, was to be a periodic ten-day cleansing regime or to be used during illness. According to macrobiotic philosophy, examples of yang foods are meat, poultry, fish, seafood, eggs, hard cheeses, and salt, whereas yin foods are alcohol, tea, coffee, sugar, milk, cream, yogurt, and most herbs and spices. Foods with a balance of yin and yang are believed to be beans, grains, nuts, seeds, fruit, and vegetables.

Michio Kushi and other Ohsawa disciples spread the word about the supposed benefits of this "macrobiotic" eating. While there are certainly some benefits in terms of the macrobiotic diet reducing the risks of obesity, raised cholesterol, high blood pressure, constipation, and some cancers, these do not compensate for the risks attached to such a restricted diet.

This diet is low in protein and high in bulk. Consequently the energy supplied by macrobiotic foods is low, which may lead to protein energy malnutrition in children up to the age of weaning, and to slow growth rates right through to adolescence and during pregnancy. Anemia is common, as a result of iron and B$_{12}$ deficiency, and there is a possible risk of rickets in children. The same benefits can be obtained, without the risks, by following far less rigid vegetarian principles or by eating a balanced omnivorous diet.

## THE DOWN SIDE

● Low in protein and high in bulk, the macrobiotic diet has many drawbacks.
• Low in fat, high in fiber.
• Too low in calories.
• Risk of nutritional deficiency, especially in iron, vitamins B$_{12}$ and D.
• Marginal protein intake.
• Unsuitable for children, for pregnant women, or for breastfeeding mothers.

# Food Combining

Dr. William Howard Hay was one of the great pioneers of the food reform movement in the early 1900s. His book, *A New Health Era*, outlined the principles of the Hay system of eating, which was based on eating only such things as he believed were intended by nature as food for man.

The fundamental principle is that starch foods and protein foods are not eaten at the same time, although "neutral" foods may be eaten with either starch or protein, but always with a gap of at least four hours between eating foods of different groups. In recent years the Hay diet has become a popular "cure-all" and its success attributed to a variety of pseudo-scientific theories. In practice I don't recommend food combining as the Way of Eating for Life, although sticking to the food-combining rules certainly has a dramatic effect on the treatment of people with a wide variety of digestive problems.

## A GUIDE TO FOOD COMBINING

Eat one starch meal, one protein meal, and one meal of mostly fruit, vegetables, and salads each day. Try to leave four hours between starch and protein meals, but if you have to nibble, try to stick to the neutral food list.

| PROTEIN | NEUTRAL | STARCH |
|---|---|---|
| Meat | All vegetables except potatoes | Potatoes |
| Poultry | All nuts except peanuts | Bread |
| Game | | Flour, oats, wheat, barley |
| Fish | Butter | Rice |
| Shellfish | Cream | Millet |
| Whole eggs | Egg yolks | Rye |
| Cheese, milk, yogurt | Sesame, sunflower, olive oils | Buckwheat |
| All fruit, except those in the starch group | All salads | Bananas, pears, papayas, grapes |
| All the legumes (lentils, dried beans) | Seeds, sprouted seeds | Dried fruit |
| Red wine | Herbs | Yogurt |
| Dry white wine | Honey | Beer |
| | Maple syrup | |
| | Gin, whisky | |

# Exclusion Diet

POSTDIET FOODS

Some people do have allergies to specific foods, such as shellfish, eggs, milk, nuts, and strawberries, but most side-effects after eating, especially those that occur between one and 24 hours later, are caused by food intolerance. The term "food intolerance," rather than "allergy," is used to describe the condition when someone shows an adverse reaction to a food, but tests for an allergy prove negative. It may result in only mild discomfort or, in some cases, may cause a severe reaction and be hard to distinguish from a true allergy.

About half the world's population does not produce the enzyme needed to digest milk, so it is hardly surprising that milk intolerance is widespread, but milk allergy—an allergic reaction to casein, which is part of milk protein—is actually quite rare, although more violent in its effects. Other foods that may produce adverse effects include coffee, tea, cocoa, chocolate, cheese, beer, sausages, yeast, red wine, wheat, and even tomatoes.

Migraine, asthma, eczema, hives, irritable bowel syndrome, colitis, Crohn's disease, hay fever, rheumatoid arthritis, and menstrual problems are just some of the disorders that may respond to dietary manipulation. Unless the particular food culprits are quite evident—in which case the obvious thing to do is avoid them—an exclusion diet (see opposite) is the best starting point.

This diet might look difficult, but you need only follow it rigorously for about two weeks, after which foods may be added back, provided you keep a record of their effect. You will soon be able to list the foods to which you are tolerant and eliminate the others.

After two weeks introduce other foods in this order: tap water, potatoes, cow's milk, yeast, tea, rye, butter, onions, eggs, oats, coffee, chocolate, barley, citrus fruits, corn, cow's cheese, white wine, shellfish, natural cow's milk yogurt, vinegar, wheat, and nuts.

Only try one new food every two days. If there is an adverse reaction, don't try it again for at least a month. Carry on adding foods from the list when any symptoms stop. Any diet that is very restricted puts your health at risk, and although it is all right to experiment on your own for a few weeks, any long-term removal of major food groups should be done only under professional guidance. When dealing with children, any major change in eating habits must be monitored by an expert nutritionist or doctor.

## THE PRINCIPLES

| FOOD TYPE | NOT ALLOWED | ALLOWED |
|---|---|---|
| *Meat, poultry* | Preserved meat, bacon, sausages, all processed meat | All other meats |
| *Fish, shellfish* | Smoked fish, shellfish | White fish |
| *Vegetables* | Potatoes, onions, sweetcorn, eggplants, sweet peppers, chilis, tomatoes | All other vegetables, salads, legumes, turnips, parsnip |
| *Fruit* | Citrus fruit, e.g. oranges, grapefruit | All other fruit (e.g. apples, bananas, pears) |
| *Cereals* | Wheat, oats, barley, rye, corn | Rice, ground rice, rice flakes, rice flour, sago, rice breakfast cereals, tapioca, millet, buckwheat, rice cakes |
| *Cooking oils* | Corn oil, vegetable oil | Sunflower oil, soy oil, safflower oil, olive oil |
| *Dairy products* | Cow's milk, butter, most margarines, cow's milk yogurt and cheese, eggs | Goat, sheep, and soy milk and products made from them, dairy and trans-fat-free margarines |
| *Beverages* | Tea, coffee (beans, instant, and decaffeinated), soft fruit drinks, orange juice, grapefruit juice, alcohol, tap water | Herbal tea (e.g. camomile), fresh fruit juices (e.g. apple, pineapple), pure tomato juice (without additives), mineral, distilled, or deionized water |
| *Miscellaneous* | Chocolates, yeast, yeast extracts, carob, sea salt, herbs, spices, artificial preservatives, colorings, small amounts of sugar or honey, flavorings, monosodium glutamate, all artificial sweeteners | |

# Convalescent Diet

NUTRITIOUS CONVALESCENT FOODS

Convalescence used to be an integral part of all medical treatment. Nutritional needs depend on the type of illness, but the general principles are to include easily digestible, nutrient-rich, and appetizing foods. The antioxidant vitamins A, C, and E, protective minerals such as zinc, and a high intake of iron to ensure good hemoglobin are essential.

Eat plenty of blackcurrants, berries, citrus fruit, and kiwi fruit, dates, oats, fish, root vegetables, broccoli, and carrots, dried fruit, garlic, cinnamon, sage, rosemary, and thyme. Cut down on refined carbohydrates, sugars, alcohol, high-bran foods, animal fats, and red meat.

Breakfasts should include porridge; yogurt with honey and pine nuts; melon; soaked dried fruits with yogurt and cinnamon; wholewheat toast; boiled, poached, or scrambled eggs. Lunches should comprise white fish; oily fish; broccoli, spinach, carrots; free-range chicken; rosemary, thyme, garlic, and sage. Evening meals should include light salads; soups made with root vegetables; barley, millet; fruit salads with almonds; low-fat cheese; avocados.

Extras should be fresh fruit, especially grapes, dates, kiwis, citrus fruit, and berries; unsweetened fresh fruit juices; vegetable juices; dried fruit; fresh nuts and seeds.

## EATING FOR LIFE

*The food entries are grouped into natural thematic sections. Each food item identifies: its nutrients; the body system(s) it benefits; conditions it can help or may exacerbate; and how the food is best eaten. The calorific value is given where relevant and, wherever possible, is quoted per 3½oz/100g. Where this is impractical, for reasons of weight or bulk, a sensible average portion is given. Super Food boxes establish supreme health-enhancers and Fast Food Fact boxes offer tips on using the pantry for first-aid.*

### KEY TO SYMBOLS

❶ Immune system
❷ Digestive system
❸ Skin, hair, and eyes
❹ Heart and circulation
❺ Nervous system
❻ Bones and muscles
❼ Respiratory system
❽ Excretory system
❾ Reproductive system

➕ Food benefits
➖ Health warning

# FRUIT

Fruit is one of the ultimate convenience foods: easy to prepare and eat, full of mouth-watering flavor and packed with vitamins, minerals, antioxidants, and fiber—all vital for health. From the seasonal delights of cherries and nectarines to the all-year-round availability of apples and pears, fruit is also very low in fat and calories, so eating plenty helps to fill us up and yet keep our weight under control.

It has long been recognized that both fruit and vegetables are beneficial for health. Current national and international recommendations to eat at least five portions of fruit and vegetables per day stem largely from research into the role of antioxidants in preventing chronic diseases such as cancer and coronary heart disease. So eating more than just "an apple a day" is a wise and healthy habit to get into.

Because fruit is so versatile it is easy to include more in our diet. Eating raw, fresh fruit offers the best vitamin value, but avoid peeling it if possible, since some vitamins are found just under the skin, and enjoying the whole fruit—including the skin—provides more fiber. Fresh fruit should, however, be well washed before eating. Choose seasonal fruit whenever possible: it is often cheaper and is likely to

LIME

provide the maximum nutrients and the most intense flavor.

When fruits are out of season, eating frozen fruit will still provide those vital vitamins and minerals, but avoid fruits that are canned in heavy syrup. Fruit juices (freshly squeezed, frozen, or concentrated) in many different flavors—from exotic peach and mango to more mundane grapefruit and apple—are good sources of vitamin C, but do not supply any fiber. They are great thirst-quenchers, but only one glass a day counts toward your goal of "five a day." Be sure to choose a "pure fruit juice" and not a "fruit drink," which comprises mainly sugar and flavoring.

The wide variety of dried fruits, from dates and mangoes to prunes and raisins, should not be overlooked for their contribution of a wide range of vitamins and minerals, including potassium, phosphorus, iron, vitamins A and B, and fiber. They are handy to eat as snacks; easily added to other foods, such as cereal and baked goods; and useful as natural sweeteners when cooked with other foods.

Eating a selection of brightly colored fruit is one of the most enjoyable ways to boost your nutritional intake.

CHERRIES

BLACKCURRANTS

## APPLES

**① ② ④ ⑥**

*Energy per average apple: 47 calories*
*Rich in vitamin C and soluble fiber*

An apple a day keeps the doctor away, but two apples a day could be a real tonic for the heart and circulation. Apples are rich in a soluble fiber, pectin, which helps the body to eliminate cholesterol and also protects against environmental pollutants. Researchers in France, Italy, and Ireland have found that two apples a day can lower cholesterol levels by up to 10 percent. The pectin joins up with heavy metals such as lead and mercury and helps the body to get rid of them. Apples also contain malic and tartaric acids, which aid digestion and are especially helpful in dealing with rich, fatty foods. The vitamin C in apples helps to boost the body's own immune defenses.

Traditionally apples have been used to treat stomach upsets, and naturopaths recommend grated apple, left to turn brown and mixed with a little honey, as an effective remedy for diarrhea. The BRAT diet (that is, bananas, rice, apples, and dry toast) is popular with doctors for the relief of diarrhea. Apples are also an important weapon in the fight against constipation because of their soluble fiber. In addition, they are ideal for people who are suffering from arthritis, rheumatism, gout, colitis, and gastroenteritis, making them an extremely versatile food.

Even the smell of apples has a calming effect and helps lower blood pressure. The sugar in apples is mostly fructose, a simple sugar that is broken down slowly and thus helps to keep blood-sugar levels on an even keel.

➕ *Good for the heart and circulation.*
➕ *Beneficial for constipation and for diarrhea.*
➕ *Best eaten raw or lightly stewed.*

### SUPER FOOD

● A couple of apples eaten the morning after the night before will help to alleviate a hangover.

## PEARS
❷ ❹

*Energy per standard portion 64 calories*
*Rich in potassium and soluble fiber*

The nutritional value of pears is often overlooked, because they are usually considered little more than a pleasant, sweet dessert fruit. In fact, pears are a good source of the soluble fiber pectin. This is not only valuable as a regulator of bowel function, but also has the specific property of helping the body to eliminate cholesterol. Pears are also a reasonable source of vitamin C, supply some vitamin A, a good amount of potassium, and a little vitamin E. Dried pears are a useful source of protein, iron, vitamin A, and vitamin C and an abundant source of potassium and fiber.

For people suffering from digestive problems or for convalescents, pears are an extremely easily digested fruit and a much more appealing alternative to bran.

➕ *Good for energy, convalescence, constipation, cholesterol lowering.*
➕ *Best eaten ripe and raw, or dried.*
➖ *Fresh pears contain a sugar-based alcohol called sorbitol, which in large amounts may cause diarrhea in a small number of susceptible people.*

## RHUBARB
❷ ❻

*Energy per 3½oz / 100g 7 calories*
*Rich in calcium*

This strange-looking plant with giant leaves and pink stems hails originally from China and Tibet, where it has been used as medicine since long before the start of the Christian era. Medicinal varieties of rhubarb, grown for their roots, rather than for their stems, were also used by the ancient Greeks to help treat chronic constipation.

Rhubarb contains small amounts of vitamins A and C, virtually no sodium, a good quantity of potassium and manganese, as well as a surprisingly large amount of calcium.

Unfortunately, the edible stems also contain oxalic acid, which interferes with the absorption of the calcium.

➕ *Good for constipation.*
➕ *Best eaten lightly stewed.*
➖ *Rhubarb leaves contain so much oxalic acid that they are seriously poisonous and must never be eaten.*
➖ *Because of its high oxalic acid content, rhubarb should not be eaten by people with, or prone to, kidney stones or gout.*

# PLUMS

❷ ❹

*Energy per standard portion 20 calories*
*Rich in potassium*

There are many varieties of plums and most of those found in Britain are hybrids of the sloe or the cherry plum. They probably originated in eastern Europe and have been known and used throughout Europe for over 2,000 years. The Japanese plum was introduced to the United States in the late seventeenth century by fruit expert Luther Burbank.

Plums contain very little vitamin C, modest amounts of vitamin A, and some vitamin E. They are, however, good sources of potassium. Dessert plums have a higher sugar and lower acid content, as well as some useful medicinal value. Sloes, wild plums from the blackthorn bush, are used to make sloe gin, a traditional country alcoholic drink that is also an excellent remedy for diarrhea.

Plums are widely used in Oriental medicine, especially the Japanese Umebushi plums, which help treat digestive disorders but taste particularly revolting.

➕ *Good for the heart and circulation and for fluid retention.*
➕ *Best eaten either very ripe and raw, or cooked.*

---

**FAST FOOD FACT**

● Wild plum jelly or jam is a soothing remedy for irritating dry coughs. For instant relief, dissolve two teaspoonfuls in a mug of hot water with the juice of a lemon and a pinch of cinnamon, and drink at bedtime.

## CHERRIES
**❶ ❻ ❽**

*Energy per 3¹/₂oz / 100g 48 calories*
*Rich in vitamin C and bioflavonoids*

Traditionally the bark of the wild cherry was used medicinally, but the dried fruit stems and the fruit themselves are an extremely effective diuretic—cherries have a reasonable potassium content and virtually no sodium. The wild cherry is pleasantly sweet and is even called the sweet cherry. Sour cherries, like morellos, are wonderful for cooking and bottling, for juice and liqueurs.

Cherries contain vitamin C and significant amounts of bioflavonoids, which makes them an excellent antioxidant food. But what adds to their value as a cancer protector is their ellagic acid, which inhibits the carcinogenic cells.

➕ *Good for the joints and for cancer protection.*
➕ *A useful diuretic.*
➕ *Best eaten fresh (the sweet cherry variety); cooked or bottled (non-dessert types).*

## APRICOTS
**❶ ❷ ❸ ❾**

DRIED APRICOTS
*Energy per 3¹/₂oz / 100g 188 calories*

FRESH APRICOTS
*Energy per 3¹/₂oz / 100g 31 calories*
*Rich in beta-carotene and iron*

Apricots contain large amounts of beta-carotene, which the body converts to vitamin A. Ripe, fresh apricots should form a regular part of the diet for anyone with infections or skin problems, or at risk of getting cancer, such as smokers.

Dried apricots are a terrific remedy for constipation, because of their high fiber content, but they are also high in sugar (so diabetics should treat them with caution), and often preserved with sulfur dioxide, which can trigger asthma attacks, so rinse them well before eating. Women of child-bearing age benefit from a few dried apricots each day, since they are a good source of iron. Their potassium also stimulates the body to get rid of excessive water and salt.

➕ *Excellent for all skin and respiratory conditions, and useful for those suffering from cancer.*
➕ *Dried apricots are good for constipation, high blood pressure, anemia, and fluid retention.*
➕ *Best eaten raw or dried.*

## NECTARINES AND PEACHES

② ④ ⑤ ⑨

NECTARINES
*Energy per standard portion 60 calories*

PEACHES
*Energy per standard portion 36 calories*
*Rich in vitamin C and iron*

Many food books describe peaches and nectarines as being different varieties of the same fruit. In fact, nectarines are no more than a genetic variation of the peach, and both are part of the *Prunus* family of prunes, plums, and apricots. The botanical name for the species is *persica*, because early botanists thought that peaches originated in Persia. Modern opinion is that the peach started life in China and was taken to Persia by early traders.

### FAST FOOD FACT

● If you are lucky enough to have a peach tree in your yard, the leaves make an excellent poultice for the treatment of boils. Soak them in boiling water until pliable, press out the surplus water and, when cool enough not to scald, apply them gently to the affected area and cover with a clean cloth.

Nutritionally there is little difference between them: both contain good amounts of vitamin C—one nectarine providing a day's requirement—small amounts of fiber, modest numbers of calories, some beta-carotene, and minerals.

Dried peaches contain far more calories but 3½oz/100g will provide almost a day's requirement of iron and one-third of your daily need of potassium. Canned peaches may taste good, but nearly all the vitamin C is lost and they are usually canned in heavy syrup so are high in calories.

Peaches and nectarines are virtually fat- and sodium-free, making them ideal for those with cholesterol and blood-pressure problems.

✛ *Good during pregnancy.*
✛ *A very gentle laxative.*
✛ *Useful for those on low-salt diets or with high cholesterol.*
✛ *Dried peaches are good for anemia, fatigue, and constipation.*
✛ *Best eaten raw, washed and ripe.*

# CITRUS FRUIT

*Prized for its vitamin C,*
*fiber, and potassium content*

Virtually unrivaled in the vitamin C stakes, citrus fruits help protect the body against infection and are a particularly good source of insoluble and soluble fiber, as well as potassium. Their tangy taste is just one of the reasons why we should eat more of these health-giving foods.

ORANGE

Of all foods with medicinal properties, citrus fruit are among the most important. Their exceptionally rich vitamin C content traditionally prevented the disease scurvy, and they offer an enormous boost to the body's natural resistance against bacteria and viruses. The US National Cancer Institute has suggested that an increased consumption of citrus fruit and juices is linked to the large reduction in the incidence of cancer of the stomach among Americans.

Millions of tons of citrus fruit are produced worldwide. Most of the fruit that we eat is grown in the Mediterranean and the United States, but the largest single producer is Brazil where, as in the United States, a large percentage of the fruit is converted to juice, concentrated, frozen, and exported to the rest of the world.

Citrus fruit are a treasure trove of nutrients and phyto-chemicals, which not only protect against disease, but are curative and health-promoting in the most positive sense.

PINK GRAPEFRUIT

## BERGAMOT

*Not to be taken internally*

Few people recognize bergamot as being a member of the citrus family. It is grown almost exclusively in the coastal area of Calabria in southern Italy, where it is used for its essential oil. This oil is extracted from the peel of the bergamot fruit and is highly fragrant, containing limonene, linalol, and bergapten.

Bergamot is widely used as a flavoring but it is most easily recognizable in the distinctive flavor of Earl Grey tea.

Bergamot oil increases the photosensitivity of the skin, which is why it is used in some sun lotions.

- ✚ *Has a highly fragrant and distinctive scent.*
- ▬ *Can produce hypersensitivity and very irritating rashes on exposure to sunlight.*
- ▬ *Should not be taken internally, but can be used in aromatherapy.*

## TANGERINES AND SATSUMAS

**① ④**

TANGERINES
*Energy per standard portion 21 calories*

SATSUMAS
*Energy per standard portion 25 calories*
*Rich in vitamin C and folate*

These fruit are both part of the mandarin family, of which satsumas, the Mediterranean mandarin, and the common mandarin are the principal hybrids. Common mandarins include tangerines, plus tangors (a hybrid of the mandarin and orange) and tangelos (a hybrid of the mandarin, grapefruit, and pomelo). Tangerines and satsumas are less acidic than lemons, limes, and grapefruits. They are still good sources of vitamin C, although they contain rather less potassium and slightly less of the B vitamins, but they do supply significant amounts of folate.

Tangerines and satsumas have the advantage of being much easier to peel than oranges so are often more acceptable to children.

- ✚ *Good for resistance and the treatment of coughs, colds, and flu.*
- ✚ *Beneficial for cancer protection.*
- ✚ *Best eaten fresh and raw, with some of the pith and membranes.*

## ORANGES

**❶ ❹**

*Energy per standard portion 59 calories*
*Rich in vitamin C and beta-carotene*

The high vitamin C content of oranges—at least when they have recently been picked or juiced—accounts for much of their benign influence on our health, because of their enormous importance in combating infection and preserving general health. Oranges also contain beta-carotene, as well as bioflavonoids in the pith and segment walls. These chemicals strengthen the walls of the tiny blood capillaries.

As a proportion of the recommended daily allowance, a glass of orange juice provides 110 percent vitamin C, 8 percent thiamin, 8 percent folic acid, 4 percent vitamin $B_6$, 4 percent magnesium, 2 percent phosphorus, and just under 2 percent protein, vitamin A, riboflavin, nicotinic acid, calcium, and iron. Drinking it with a meal can increase iron absorption by up to two-and-a-half times.

The fruit, flowers, and peel of oranges have long been used in herbal medicine. The peel contains hesperidine and limonene, which are used in the treatment of chronic bronchitis. Tea made from the dried flowers is a mild stimulant.

### FAST FOOD FACT

● The essential oil neroli, which is made from orange blossom, is widely used in aromatherapy as a mild sedative. Five drops in 1fl oz/25ml of carrier oil can be massaged into the back, neck, and shoulders to relieve tension and encourage sleep. Neroli is also one of the main constituents in eau-de-Cologne, which, when dabbed on the brow and the temples, can bring instant relief from a headache.

➕ *Excellent for combating infection and improving circulation.*

➕ *Orange juice is beneficial for heart disease, high blood pressure, and fluid retention.*

➕ *Best eaten fresh and raw, with some of the pith and membrane.*

➖ *Some migraine-sufferers are sensitive to one or other citrus fruit, and even inhaling the oily zest from the peel can trigger an attack. If you can't buy organic or unwaxed fruit, scrub the skin under hot water before adding the peel to food or drink.*

# LEMONS

**1 2 4 7**

*Energy per standard portion 1 calorie*
*Rich in vitamin C and bioflavonoids*

Lemons earned their reputation as a cure for scurvy long before vitamin C was actually identified. They have an abundant supply of this vitamin—3½oz/100g, providing more than a day's dose—as well as small amounts of some B vitamins, vitamin E, substantial quantities of potassium, magnesium, calcium, and phosphorus and the important trace minerals copper, zinc, iron, and manganese. They also activate the immune system by stimulating white corpuscle activity.

Lemons are rich in bioflavonoids, limonene, and mucilage, the latter being beneficial to the lining of the digestive tract and stomach. Lemon juice can also act as a stimulant to the pancreas and liver. Its powerful antibacterial activity makes it first choice as a gargle or mouthwash for sore throats, mouth ulcers, and gingivitis, diluted half-and-half with hot water.

✚ *Boost the immune system.*
✚ *Helpful for digestive problems, mouth ulcers, and gum problems.*
✚ *Best eaten fresh and raw or used as juice.*

## SUPER FOOD

● Traditionally, lemons have always been used for infections of the respiratory tract. Hot lemon taken with one teaspoon of honey at bedtime is a classic remedy for coughs and colds.

## FAST FOOD FACTS

● Lemon juice applied neat with a Q-tip to pus-filled spots is a powerful bactericide and is particularly effective for acne; diluted half-and-half with hot water it makes an excellent facial wash. It can also be applied directly to cold sores or the rash of shingles, provided that the skin is unbroken.

● Chilblains can be relieved by rubbing the surface of the affected area with a slice of lemon dipped in coarse sea salt—but only on unbroken skin, or this will hurt.

## LIMES
❶ ❹

*Energy per standard portion 24 calories
Rich in vitamin C and bioflavonoids*

These are the most acid citrus fruit and, although they contain more vitamin C than grapefruit, they have slightly less than oranges and lemons. They are grown primarily for their juice, which is used as a flavoring for other foods, particularly drinks. Like other citrus fruit limes contain high amounts of bioflavonoids.

Lime juice can be used, like lemon juice, for its medicinal properties.

➕ *Good for resistance and the treatment of coughs, colds, and flu.*
➕ *Beneficial for cancer protection.*
➕ *Best used as juice.*

## GRAPEFRUIT
❶ ❹

*Energy per standard portion 24 calories
Rich in vitamin C, potassium,
and beta-carotene*

Grapefruit contain a high level of vitamin C—it is estimated that one grapefruit supplies nearly 60 percent of the recommended daily allowance in the American diet—and plenty of useful potassium. Pink or red grapefruit are marginally higher in vitamin C than white ones.

Grapefruit are also well supplied with a number of carotenoids, including beta-carotene, and with pectin and bioflavonoids in the white pith and the cell walls dividing the sections. So make sure that you eat the whole fruit in order to gain the maximum benefit.

➕ *Useful for resistance and circulatory problems.*
➕ *Good for sore throats and bleeding gums.*
➕ *Best eaten fresh and raw, with some of the pith and membranes.*

# BERRY FRUIT

*Prized for its vitamin C and soluble fiber content*

Berries are those surprisingly flavorsome little fruits that are best eaten fresh, straight from the vine, for maximum flavor and nutrient value. They are nutritionally important for their large amounts of vitamin C, useful amounts of the soluble fiber, pectin, and—although they contain very small amounts of some minerals—these minerals are well absorbed into the body, because of the presence of the vitamin C.

CRANBERRIES

Many of these berries—for example, blackberries, blueberries, cranberries, gooseberries, raspberries, strawberries, and, less commonly, currants— still grow wild in various countries. They are very ancient fruits and were traditionally used by travelers in the past as sources of vitamin C to prevent scurvy.

BLUEBERRI

Some berries, such as cranberries and blackcurrants, have useful medicinal purposes. They provide the maximum amount of vitamin C when eaten fresh, but since many berries are also acidic, even when they are preserved by freezing or canning they still supply a large proportion of the recommended daily amount of vitamin C.

Due to their bright colors and significant quantities of pectin, many berries make good jams and jellies. They are also popular in sauces, puddings, added to baked goods and made into concentrates for drinks.

STRAWBERRIES

# BLACKBERRIES

❶ ❷ ❹

*Energy per 3$^1/_2$oz / 100g 25 calories*
*Rich in vitamins C and E*

Blackberries are extremely rich in vitamin E (although wild berries have a higher concentration than the cultivated varieties). This makes them extremely useful in both the prevention and treatment of heart and circulatory problems. They are also a good source of vitamin C, which makes them a strong antioxidant, protective against cancers, degenerative diseases, and infections. Blackberries also contain useful amounts of potassium and enough of the soluble fiber, pectin, to make a significant contribution to the minimum daily requirement.

Blackberry leaves are very astringent, containing large amounts of tannin, which explains many of their traditional uses. Chopped and used as a tea, they make an excellent mouthwash for gum problems and infections like gingivitis, as well as an effective gargle for sore throats; and 1oz/30g of dried leaves steeped in 3 cups/600ml of boiling water is also an excellent remedy for diarrhea—two cups per day is usually sufficient.

➕ *Good for the heart, circulation, and skin problems.*

➕ *Beneficial for diarrhea.*

➕ *The leaves are useful for scalds, gum disease, and sore throats.*

➕ *Best eaten raw or lightly stewed; combine well with apples.*

## THE AMERICAN BLACKBERRY

● Sometimes called the fingerberry or black haw, this species contains considerably more tannic acid than the English variety. Traditionally it has been used as a fluid extract of dried bark or root, and as a syrup to treat diarrhea and even dysentery.

## FAST FOOD FACT

● A poultice of blackberry leaves macerated in boiling water and left to cool is a traditional remedy for scalds—the tannins in the leaves act as an antiseptic and so help prevent secondary infection from occurring.

## BLUEBERRIES
② ④ ⑧

*Energy per 3¹/₂oz / 100g 30 calories*
*Rich in vitamin C*

Nutritionally speaking, blueberries are not very exciting, though they do contain reasonable amounts of vitamin C and small amounts of vitamins $B_1$, beta-carotene, and potassium. It is their natural chemicals, however, that make them valuable in medicinal terms. Blueberries contain the antibacterial anthocyanosides, which have a tonic effect on blood vessels and make them a useful aid in the treatment of varicose veins, cystitis, and other urinary infections.

When the berries are dried, the concentration of tannins and other antibacterials is substantially increased, which probably explains the effectiveness of Scandinavian dried blueberry soup as a treatment for diarrhea.

✚  *Good for food poisoning and diarrhea, and as an antibacterial.*
✚  *Beneficial for cystitis and other urinary infections, and also for varicose veins.*
✚  *Best eaten raw, or cooked in the traditional blueberry muffin.*
➖  *Their fruit-sugar content can cause diarrhea, if eaten in excess.*

## RASPBERRIES
① ② ④ ⑤

*Energy per standard portion 15 calories*
*Rich in vitamin C and soluble fiber*

Like grapes, raspberries should be on every hospital menu. This delicious fruit is a rich source of vitamin C—3¹/₂oz/100g provides 50 percent of the US recommended daily allowance. Raspberries are also a useful source of the soluble fiber, pectin, and contain small amounts of calcium, potassium, iron, and magnesium—all vital to the convalescent, as well as to those suffering from heart problems, fatigue, or depression, and all well absorbed, thanks to the vitamin C.

Herbalists value raspberries for their cooling effect, which is useful in feverish conditions. Naturally astringent, raspberries can do you good the entire length of your digestive tract, helping to counter spongy, diseased gums, upset stomachs, and diarrhea.

✚  *Good for the immune system, cancer protection, and for mouth problems.*
✚  *Best eaten fresh.*

## CRANBERRIES

❶ ❽

*Energy per standard portion 11 calories*
*Rich in vitamin C*

Cranberries are one of the very few fruits native to North America, and for centuries the Native North Americans used these extraordinary berries as both food and medicine.

They bathed their wounds in cranberry juice, and their medicine men made cranberry poultices to draw out the poison from arrow injuries. Thanks to the vitamin C in cranberries, early American settlers avoided the terrors of scurvy, and it was not long before American whalers were carrying barrels of cranberries, just as English ships carried limes. To this day Americans celebrate the fourth Thursday of November with a Thanksgiving meal made up of turkey, cornbread, sweet potatoes, pumpkin pie, and, of course, cranberry sauce.

For decades American folklore has advocated the use of cranberry juice in both the treatment and prevention of acute and chronic recurring attacks of cystitis, and a number of scientific studies have now confirmed this ancient native wisdom. It has always been thought that the acidity of

cranberry juice, together with its hippuric acid, produced its anti-bacterial effect, but it is now almost certain that this is not its most important constituent. Cranberries contain a component that covers the walls of the bladder, kidneys, and interconnecting tubing, which prevents bacteria from attaching themselves to these sensitive tissues, where they would normally live and multiply. It has now been shown that a glass of cranberry juice a day is ten times as effective at killing urinary bacteria as conventional antibiotics.

Other research has further shown that most sufferers of chronic urinary infection stay infection-free as long as they drink one glass of cranberry juice a day. Overall these results are better than those that are achieved using conventional antibiotic treatment.

- ✚ *Beneficial for cystitis and other urinary infections.*
- ✚ *Good for boosting the immune system.*
- ✚ *Best taken as unsweetened juice.*

# STRAWBERRIES

**① ④ ⑤ ⑥**

*Energy per standard portion 27 calories*
*Rich in vitamin C and soluble fiber*

There is a popular myth that anyone with arthritis should avoid strawberries because they are acidic, but nothing could be further from the truth. Linnaeus, the great Swedish botanist, recommended strawberries as a perfect cure for arthritis, gout, and rheumatism. He spoke from personal experience; he cured himself of gout by eating almost nothing but strawberries, morning and night. This agreeable cure probably works because strawberries help to eliminate the joint-irritating uric acid from the body.

Strawberries are reputed to reduce high blood pressure and are recommended in traditional European medicine for the elimination of kidney stones. They contain modest amounts of iron and, because of their extremely high vitamin C content, the iron is well absorbed, making them useful in both the prevention and treatment of anemia and fatigue— 3½oz/100g of strawberries will give you almost twice your vitamin C needs for a day.

Strawberries are rich in the soluble fiber, pectin, which helps in the elimination of cholesterol. This, combined with their powerful antioxidant properties, makes them highly effective against heart and circulatory disease. There is also a growing body of evidence that claims that these delicious fruits have antiviral properties, too. This is one medicine that does not need a spoonful of sugar to help it down. These wonderful berries should be eaten on their own, or at the start of a meal, in order to achieve their best therapeutic value.

## SUPER FOOD

● A few strawberries each day during the season is the cheapest, and most delicious, health insurance you will ever buy.

➕ *Good for cancer protection, gout, arthritis, and anemia.*
➕ *Best eaten fresh and ripe.*
➖ *May cause severe allergic reactions in some people.*

## GOOSEBERRIES

**❶ ❷ ❽**

*Energy per 3¹/₂oz / 100g 40 calories*
*Rich in vitamin C and malic acid*

Gooseberries are an excellent source of vitamin C, 3¹/₂oz/100g of the fresh berries providing well over one-third the US recommended daily allowance. Because of their high acid content, little of the vitamin C is lost in cooking or canning, making them one of the few canned fruits with a significant vitamin C content.

It is a great shame that gooseberries have acquired a rather strange reputation—"playing gooseberry," "babies found under the gooseberry bush"—for they are not only health-giving but delicious, whether eaten raw, cooked in pies, made into sauces, or even turned into traditional English country wine. Gooseberries are especially popular in Britain and France, and the French name *groseille à maquereau* comes from the delicious gooseberry sauce that the French serve with mackerel. In Britain the same sauce is traditionally served with fatty meats, especially goose. The origin of the name, however, has nothing to do with geese, but comes from the French root *groseille*.

Due to their high content of malic acid, gooseberries are useful in the treatment of any urinary infections; they help to acidify urine without causing undue gastric discomfort. Gooseberries are also a useful source of soluble fiber, which makes them a very palatable remedy to take for constipation.

### FAST FOOD FACT

● For a really bad cold, mix one teaspoon of gooseberry jam, one teaspoon of blackcurrant jam, and the juice of half a lemon in a mug of boiling water and drink three times a day.

✚ *Good for building up natural resistance.*
✚ *Beneficial for constipation.*
✚ *Useful for urinary infections.*
✚ *Best eaten raw (dessert varieties) or lightly stewed (culinary varieties).*

## REDCURRANTS
**❶**

*Energy per 3½oz/100g 21 calories*
*Rich in vitamin C and potassium*

The redcurrant is brother to the blackcurrant, but there are considerable differences in their nutritional value. This plant grows quite happily in most situations and is extremely hardy, surviving the climates of such diverse locations as Britain, northern Europe, the United States, and Siberia. It is often found growing wild in hedges and ditches, where the fruit is always red, although cultivated varieties may produce whitecurrants (which will not contain any vitamin A).

Although containing only a quarter of the vitamin C of blackcurrants 3½oz/100g of redcurrants will still supply almost the US recommended daily allowance. This makes them valuable for improving the natural function of the immune system. Although when cooked they lose some vitamin C, used as jellies, juices, or stewed with other fruits, redcurrants can make an important contribution to the diet of a recovering invalid. Redcurrants also supply modest amounts of iron and fiber and quite a large amount of potassium, none of which is lost during cooking.

Herbalists have traditionally recommended redcurrant juice as a temperature-lowering drink for anyone with a fever. The British tradition of eating redcurrant jelly with "high" game (game birds hung till they begin to putrefy) was thought to protect against harmful bacteria, because of its high acid content.

### FAST FOOD FACT

● Redcurrant jelly is antiseptic and, if it is applied to a burn after cooling it with plenty of cold water, will ease the pain and prevent blistering.

✚ *Good for strengthening the immune system.*
✚ *The juice is a cooling, refreshing drink for fevers.*
✚ *Best eaten raw, stewed, as jelly or juice.*

## BLACKCURRANTS

❶ ❷ ❹ ❺

*Energy per 3¹/₂oz / 100g 28 calories*
*Rich in vitamin C*

Blackcurrants are an exceptionally rich source of vitamin C, containing four times as much as an equivalent weight of oranges—2oz/60g gives you 60mg of this vital vitamin, which is particularly stable in blackcurrants. The vitamin C in this tiny berry is a powerful antioxidant, protecting against heart disease, circulatory problems, and all manner of infections. But blackcurrants also contain substantial amounts of potassium but very little sodium, so they help with water retention and are also useful in the treatment of high blood pressure.

### FAST FOOD FACT

● Blackcurrant leaves have important medical uses too, containing volatile oils, tannins, and still more vitamin C. Use them as a tea to make a gargle for the relief of mouth ulcers. Drinking this can have a direct effect on the adrenal glands, stimulating the sympathetic nervous system and thereby helping to relieve problems of stress and anxiety.

Pigments called anthocyanosides in their purple-black skins have bactericidal qualities and an anti-inflammatory action, both of which are put to good use in the country remedy for sore throats—hot blackcurrant juice sipped very slowly. An easy way to make this is to simmer half a cup of blackcurrants in two cups of hot water for 10 minutes, then strain and add some honey. Or add boiling water to one teaspoon of blackcurrant jelly. This powerful antibacterial effect is valuable in treating and preventing food poisoning, because many of the pathogens that trigger stomach upsets are destroyed by the anthocyanosides.

✚ *Beneficial for building up a strong immune system, for colds, flu, and sore throats.*
✚ *Useful for cancer protection, fluid retention, high blood pressure, stress, and anxiety.*
✚ *Good for diarrhea and for food poisoning.*
✚ *Best drunk as juice, eaten as jelly, or lightly stewed with other fruits.*

# TROPICAL FRUIT

*Prized for its vitamins A, C, and fiber content*

Many tropical fruits grown in warm climates have exquisite flavors when fresh and ripe, and add wonderful variety and color to meals and snacks. Because they hail from different tropical countries around the world, they are now available in supermarkets year-round as imported fresh fruit. For the best flavor, nutritional value, and quality, buy tropical fruit when it is nearly ripe and allow it to mature naturally. Many fruits, such as the banana and mango, have been grown extensively since ancient times, while others—such as the kiwi, papaya, and guava—have become widely available only in recent years.

The brightly colored, deep-yellow- and orange-colored fruits are rich sources of vitamin A. They vary in the amount of vitamin C that they contain, but the small, popular kiwi fruit, for example, is in fact much richer in vitamin C than an orange. Bananas and other tropical fruit are well known for their potassium content, and many fruits provide small amounts of other minerals and are also useful sources of fiber.

Some tropical fruit, such as pineapples, mangoes, and guavas, are widely available as canned fruit, but try to find those that have been canned in juice rather than very heavy syrup; or discard the syrup, which mainly comprises added sugar.

WATERMELON

## GRAPES

① ② ③ ⑤ ⑥ ⑧

*Energy per standard portion 60 calories*
*Rich in aromatic compounds*

The use of grapes for the production of raisins and wine was widespread in the earliest times. *Vitis vinifera* is the species at the root of most modern grape production. It was taken across to the New World by Columbus in 1492 and again by the Spanish and Portuguese who went to both North and South America. The United States is now the world's second-largest producer of grapes and raisins.

Grapes are a uniquely nourishing, strengthening, cleansing, and regenerative food, ideal in convalescence, and useful for anemia, fatigue, and disorders such as arthritis, gout, and rheumatism, which may result from poor elimination.

Their nutritive powers were confirmed by Mahatma Gandhi, who drank grape juice during his marathon fasts, and grape monofasts have since been used for a wide range of ailments, including skin problems, disorders of the urinary system, arthritis, and gout. A two-day monofast on grapes every ten days is recommended for those wanting to lose weight. And many naturopaths believe that grapes should be eaten on their own, not as part of a meal, since they ferment rapidly in the stomach. Chewing grapes is also recommended for infected gums.

Grapes contain an enormous number of aromatic compounds—far more than all other fruit. The most important of these are the astringent tannins, flavones, red anthocyanins, linalol, geraniol, and nerol. These are believed to provide grapes with their cancer-protective value.

➕ *Good for convalescence, weight loss, anemia, and fatigue.*
➕ *Useful for cancer protection.*
➕ *Best eaten raw.*
➖ *Since most grapes are sprayed incessantly during cultivation, it is vital to wash them very carefully in warm running water.*

BANANA

PLANTAIN

## BANANAS AND PLANTAINS

② ④ ⑤ ⑨

BANANAS
*Energy per standard portion 95 calories*

PLANTAIN
*Energy per 3¹/₂oz / 100g 117 calories*
*Rich in potassium, vitamin B₆, and folic acid*

Bananas are one of nature's miracle foods and are full of nutrients: the perfect fast food, which come in their own packaging. Slimmers generally avoid bananas in the mistaken belief that they are fattening, but, at only 95 calories per fruit, they represent excellent nutritional value.

The starch in bananas is not easily digested, which is why they should only be eaten ripe (when the skin turns a speckled brown), when most of the starch has turned to sugar. The starch in plantains can cause considerable discomfort if they are eaten raw, but this is avoided by cooking them. Ripe bananas are good for the treatment of both constipation and diarrhea, as well as

helping to eliminate cholesterol from the body. Plantains are very rich in the specific starch that is highly beneficial in the treatment and prevention of stomach ulcers. They have been used as a prime energy source and staple food in India, Southeast Asia, South America, and East Africa for centuries.

The high potassium content in bananas helps prevent cramp and, combined with the easily available energy, means they are the ideal snack for those engaged in active sports. One banana contains just over a quarter of the daily requirement of vitamin B₆, so they should also be eaten by women suffering from PMS.

➕ *Good for physically active people and for raised cholesterol.*

➕ *Beneficial for stomach ulcers, convalescents, chronic fatigue syndrome, exhaustion, and mononucleosis.*

➕ *Bananas best eaten ripe and raw; plantains best eaten underripe and cooked.*

### FAST FOOD FACT

● A few banana skins buried in the soil around your raspberry canes guarantee succulent, beautifully colored fruit, thanks to their magnesium content.

HONEYDEW MELON

WATERMELON

# MELON

② ⑥ ⑧

HONEYDEW MELON
*Energy per standard portion 29 calories*

WATERMELON
*Energy per standard portion 62 calories*
*Rich in vitamin C and potassium*

Melons belong to the same group of plants as cucumbers, pumpkins, squashes, and gourds. They have been cultivated in Asia since the most ancient of times and were a valued fruit to the Egyptians, Greeks, and Romans. They were first cultivated in western Europe by the French and have been used by herbalists since the sixteenth century. The serpent melon, which is extremely long, is eaten raw or pickled and is the "cucumber" described by Isaiah, but it is the watermelon, originally native to the East Indies and Africa, that is the great refresher and has long been used medicinally. The seeds were believed to be a good treatment for worms and urinary infections.

Melons are a cooling, delicious treat in hot weather, and a large slice of crunchy pink watermelon beats any canned fizzy drink for refreshment. Watermelon—or a tea that has been made by simmering its seeds in water for 30 minutes—has long been recommended in traditional medicine as a natural remedy for kidney and bladder problems. In fact, all forms of melon are mildly stimulating to the kidneys and gently laxative, making them useful for those suffering from gout or constipation.

✚ *Good for mild constipation, urinary problems, gout, and arthritis.*

✚ *Best eaten raw, ripe, and on its own.*

## FAST FOOD FACT

● Naturopaths maintain that melons of all kinds should be eaten on their own, or at least at the start of a meal, since they ferment rapidly in the stomach. One of the most traditional naturopathic cleansing regimes is a two-day monofast on melons of any kind—making a delightful summer break for the whole system.

## PINEAPPLES
❶ ❷ ❹

*Energy per standard portion 33 calories*
*Rich in fiber and bromelain*

Although pineapple offers little nutritionally except for modest amounts of vitamin C, its fiber content and its ability to break down blood clots make it an excellent heart-protector. The juice of fresh pineapples is an effective folk medicine for sore throats—an instant gargle—and was once a favorite herbal remedy for diphtheria. Some of its therapeutic compounds probably survive commercial processing, but fresh ripe pineapple or freshly extracted juice must be your first choice.

✚ *Good for digestive problems, fevers, sore throats, and generalized soft-tissue injuries.*
✚ *An excellent heart-protector.*
✚ *Best eaten very ripe, or juiced.*

### SUPER FOOD

● The enzyme bromelain, present only in fresh pineapples, helps dissolve the congealed blood cells that cause bruising—fresh pineapple has long replaced raw steak as a treatment for black eyes in boxing.

## GUAVAS
❶ ❷ ❹

*Energy per standard portion 23 calories*
*Rich in vitamin C and soluble fiber*

The guava (especially the pink-fleshed one) is an extremely rich source of vitamin C—one average fruit supplies over three days' worth of the minimum US requirement. The vitamin C content is at its peak in green mature fruit, but starts to fall the more ripe the fruit becomes. Guavas also contain useful amounts of nicotinic acid, phosphorus, and calcium, together with plenty of good soluble fiber. Even canned guavas, which can lose up to one-third of their vitamin C content during processing, retain their fiber content, but don't use the heavy sugar syrup. The popular guava nectar is a mixture of 25 percent fruit pureé with 10 percent sugar, and 65 percent water.

✚ *Beneficial for boosting immunity, reducing cholesterol, and for constipation.*
✚ *Heart- and cancer-protective.*
✚ *Best eaten raw and slightly underripe.*

## PAPAYAS

❶ ❷ ❸ ❹

*Energy per standard portion 50 calories*
*Rich in vitamin C, fiber, and beta-carotene*

This delicious, nutritious tropical fruit was originally a native of southern Mexico and Costa Rica. Thanks to the Spaniards, who introduced papayas to Manila in the middle part of the sixteenth century, it is now grown throughout the tropics. The world's biggest producer by far is the United States, where most of the fruit is grown in Hawaii.

Nutritionally this is a very important plant food in developing countries, because the papaya produces fruit throughout the year and is an excellent source of vitamin C. Like most other orange-colored fruit and vegetables, it is also a wonderful source of beta-carotene, which is converted by the body into vitamin A. Papayas are therefore excellent for treating skin problems as well as for boosting the body's immune defense mechanisms.

They are also a useful food for invalids, the flesh being soft and easy to chew. But canned papaya is nutritionally poor compared with the fresh fruit, most of its vitamin C and more than half its beta-carotene being lost during the canning process.

With 3g of fiber in an average fruit, papaya also helps reduce cholesterol levels as well as maintaining regular bowel function. Their most important constituent is an enzyme called papain, which is a great aid to digestion, although present in larger quantities in the unripe fruit. In South American cooking meat is often wrapped in papaya leaves to produce tender and succulent dishes.

Papaya seeds make a spicy flavoring when added to pickles, vinegars, and oils; they are also a traditional remedy for worms. And the leaves have been used to encourage the rapid healing of wounds, boils, and leg ulcers.

➕ *Good for digestive problems.*
➕ *Beneficial for the skin and for an improved immune system.*
➕ *Best eaten raw and ripe.*

### SUPER FOOD

● An average papaya fruit supplies twice the minimum daily need of vitamin C and well over a quarter of the vitamin A.

## MANGOES

❶ ❸

*Energy per standard portion 86 calories*
*Rich in vitamins A, C, E, and fiber*

Brimful of nutrients, one average mango provides more than a day's requirement of vitamin C, two-thirds of your vitamin A, nearly half your vitamin E, almost a quarter of your fiber, as well as useful contributions of potassium, iron, and nicotinic acid. It is this great combination of antioxidants, in a very easily digestible form, that should put the mango on everybody's weekly shopping list. There are many varieties, but my favorite is the small, exceptionally sweet mango that comes from Pakistan, which unfortunately has a short season.

In their native India mangoes are part of the way of life and are eaten throughout the year—in the hot season as drinks made from pulped mangoes, to replace body fluids, especially when they are strained and mixed with salt, molasses, and cumin to make panna.

When mangoes are cheap and plentiful, use them to make milkshakes, pie fillings, and sauces, or turn them into jam.

The easiest way to serve a fresh mango is to slice off the sides as close to the stone as possible. Then, with a sharp knife, score the inside of the flesh in a criss-cross pattern. Turn the whole segment inside out and you are left with small cubes of mango looking like a porcupine, which can then be chewed off. The middle section with the stone can be peeled and then chewed or sliced off.

---

### SUPER FOOD

● In Ayurvedic medicine mango pulp is used to treat high blood pressure and diabetes, the antiseptic twigs to replace toothbrushes for oral hygiene, the bark as a treatment for diarrhea, and even the seed is made into a powder that is used in the treatment of vaginal discharge.

---

➕ *Good for convalescence, skin problems, the immune system, and cancer protection.*

➕ *Best eaten raw.*

➖ *The mango belongs to the same family as poison ivy, and its peel, especially before it is fully ripe, can be highly irritant and may cause a severe reaction.*

## KIWI FRUIT

❶ ❷ ❸

*Energy per standard portion 29 calories*
*Rich in vitamin C, fiber, and potassium*

The kiwi is not just a pretty face in a *nouvelle cuisine* dish. This little fruit with its shabby fur coat is a surprising treasury of nutritional riches. It originally came from China, then growers in New Zealand popularized the fruit, so it became known thereafter as the kiwi fruit, after the country's national emblem, the kiwi bird.

The kiwi fruit contains almost twice as much vitamin C as an orange and more fiber than an apple. One kiwi fruit gives you twice as much vitamin C as you need for a day. Compared with other fruit it is unusual in that its vitamin C content remains very stable and, although there are some losses soon after harvesting, 90 percent of it is still present in the fruit after six months in store.

The kiwi fruit is also particularly rich in potassium, of which Western diets, which are high in sodium from processed foods, can be dangerously short. Deficiency of this mineral, which is vital to every single cell in our body, can lead to high blood pressure, depression, fatigue, and poor digestion. The average kiwi fruit supplies about 250mg of potassium, but only about 4mg of sodium.

When buying kiwi fruit, choose those that are soft enough to yield to gentle pressure. They can be stored in the refrigerator—and should be peeled just before eating.

The fiber content of kiwis and their particular type of mucilage make them an excellent, but extremely gentle, laxative. This makes them ideal fruit for the elderly, who are frequently deficient in vitamin C and suffer from chronic constipation. Kiwis also contain an enzyme called actinidin, an efficient aid to digestion which is similar in action to the papain found in papaya.

✚ *Good for the immune system, skin, and digestive problems.*
✚ *Best eaten raw—slice the top off the kiwi like a boiled egg and eat with a teaspoon.*

# DRIED FRUIT
*Prized for its mineral and fiber content*

There is now a wide variety of dried fruit available, from the familiar raisin to the more exotic mango. They provide very concentrated sources of instant energy, so they are  a popular snack with athletes, walkers, and mountaineers. But not only are they good energy providers, they also contain significant amounts of iron, potassium, and selenium, and small amounts of certain other minerals, as well as fiber and vitamin

RAISINS

A (from yellow/orange dried fruit).

Dried fruits can make a significant contribution to relieving anemia, because of their high iron content; they can also be very helpful for those suffering from constipation, since their fiber content makes them a useful laxative.

Due to the sweet flavor and vital nutrients of dried fruit, many parents are slowly recognizing them as much more valuable foods for their children than candies. However, their stickiness means that they can give rise to dental caries, so they should be eaten in moderation as a snack. Dried fruits are also extremely useful chopped up in salads, stewed as a compote, or made into delicious sauces to serve with savory dishes or meat. They make excellent substitutes for sugar in baked goods, helping you to reduce—or even eliminate—the sugar content in many recipes.

PRUNES

## DATES

❷ ❹ ❺ ❾

FRESH DATES
*Energy per 3¹/₂oz / 100g 96 calories*

DRIED DATES
*Energy per 3¹/₂oz / 100g 248 calories*
*Rich in iron and potassium*

Dates have been cultivated throughout the Middle East for at least 5,000 years and form an extremely important food crop in this region of the world. They can be used as substitutes for sugar, as a staple food, and even for making fermented alcoholic drinks. Dried dates can even be ground into flour.

Fresh dates are much lower in calories than dried; they also contain modest amounts of vitamin C, but there is virtually none in the dried variety. However, it is the minerals in dates that are most interesting, especially their iron content, which seems to be little appreciated beyond the East. One or two date varieties are very poor sources of iron, but the vast majority make highly significant contributions. This, together with their easily available energy, makes them an excellent nutrient for those with anemia and illnesses that produce chronic fatigue. All dates are a reasonable source of fiber and a rich source of potassium. Though they contain only small amounts of the B vitamins, they do, however, provide reasonable amounts of folate.

Arabs traditionally eat dried dates with tea or coffee, but they also mix them with buttermilk or thick yogurt, making a dish of excellent nutritional value. A dessert made with compressed dried dates sprinkled with sesame seeds adds polyunsaturated fatty acids and proteins, making this delicious snack into a virtual meal.

✚ *Excellent for anemia, postviral and chronic fatigue syndromes.*

✚ *Beneficial for constipation.*

✚ *Best eaten as a snack or as an appetizer before meals.*

### FAST FOOD FACT

● Suffering from a lackluster love life? Throughout the Middle East dates are considered a highly potent sexual stimulant.

## PRUNES

❷ ❹ ❺

*Energy per standard portion 160 calories*
*Rich in potassium, iron, and fiber*

Prunes are the dried fruit of a specific variety of plum tree, which most famously grows around the small French town of Agen below Bordeaux. Prunes have an ancient heritage, dating back to the Crusaders, who brought them to Britain from the Middle East, but it was almost certainly the Arabs who planted the first *pruneaux d'Agen*—a label with as much history as the *Appelation Contrôlée* of any fine wine. But today California produces twice as many prunes as the rest of the world put together—70 percent of the total supply.

### SUPER FOOD

● If you are seriously trying to reduce your fat intake, use puréed prunes as a substitute for fat when baking. This can be used as a direct replacement for butter, margarine, or oil. Because of its natural sweetness, you can reduce the sugar content of most cake recipes, too.

Prunes are rich in potassium, making them valuable for those with high blood pressure, rich in fiber and iron, and also contain useful amounts of niacin, vitamin B$_6$, and vitamin A. They are an excellent source of energy, being easily digested and producing 160 calories per 3½oz/100g. They also contain a chemical (hydroxyphenylisatin) that stimulates the smooth muscle of the large bowel, making this dried fruit a very gentle laxative without any purgative action.

➕ *Good for constipation, high blood pressure, fatigue, and lethargy.*
➕ *Best eaten as they are, soaked, or used in cooking; prune juice is highly nutritious.*
➖ *Commercially produced prunes may be treated with sulfur and coated with mineral oil—remove these additives by cleaning in several washes of warm water.*

## RAISINS

❷ ❹ ❺

*Energy per standard portion 82 calories*
*Rich in natural sugars, fiber, and potassium*

Raisins are dried grapes, the very best of which are allowed to dry naturally on the vine. Traditionally raisins are laid out on earth floors and the bunches turned every 7–10 days for about three weeks. Modern production methods in Australia and California use covered, open-sided sheds and mechanized harvesting to cut the vines below the clusters of grapes, so that the fruit begins to dehydrate in the vineyard.

All the nutritional benefits of grapes are concentrated into raisins, making them a wonderful store of instant energy—3½oz/100g of raisins contains almost 2½oz/70g of natural sugars, glucose, and fructose. They are therefore an ideal high-energy food for athletes, walkers, mountaineers, and anyone suffering from chronic fatigue.

Unlike high-sugar confectionery, raisins are rich in other nutrients: fiber (to help reduce cholesterol and improve bowel function); iron (3½oz/100g providing more than 25 percent of the recommended daily allowance for women); selenium; and a huge amount of potassium (which prevents fluid retention and helps reduce blood pressure). Raisins also contain small amounts of vitamin A, and small but significant quantities of the B vitamins.

- ⊕ *Good for high blood pressure, fluid retention, low energy, anemia, and for constipation.*
- ⊕ *Best eaten well washed as a snack, or added to salads or fruit dishes.*
- ⊖ *Commercially produced raisins may be treated with sulfur and coated with mineral oil—remove these additives by cleaning in several washes of warm water.*

**SUPER FOOD**

● The combination of good, quickly available calories and B vitamins make raisins the perfect snack for all those who are suffering from depression, anxiety, and nervous irritability.

## FIGS

❶ ❷ ❹ ❾

FRESH FIGS
*Energy per 3¹/₂oz / 100g  43 calories*

DRIED FIGS
*Energy per 3¹/₂oz / 100g  213 calories*
*Rich in beta-carotene and fiber*

Figs have been valued by humanity since the earliest recorded times. Adam and Eve used fig leaves and there are many other biblical references to figs, testifying to their value as food, medicine, and symbol of plenty. In ancient Greece, Olympic athletes were fed vast quantities of figs to build up their stamina. Hindus consider the fig tree to be sacred, and one fig variety, the banyan tree, is widely used in Ayurvedic medicine.

Modern science shows that figs are a rich source of benzaldehyde, an anticancer agent. They also contain healing enzymes, flavonoids, and an enzyme known as ficin, which aids the digestion by tenderizing protein foods. All in all, figs are a wonderful source of easily digested nutrients, including iron, potassium, beta-carotene, both soluble and insoluble fiber, and energy. In many parts of the East and Asia, figs have the bonus of being regarded as a powerful aphrodisiac. Fresh and dried figs, as well as the traditional syrup of figs, are excellent laxatives.

✚ *Good for energy, constipation, digestive problems, anemia, and cancer protection.*

✚ *Best eaten ripe and raw when fresh; dried figs can be eaten either as they are, or soaked to form part of a dried fruit compote.*

### FAST FOOD FACTS

● You can use figs to treat boils and abscesses—bake a fresh fig in the oven for half an hour, cut it in half and apply the warm paste over the inflamed area to draw the boil to a head.

● And for a wart cure that works you can squeeze a milky juice out of a broken leaf or stem and paint it onto your wart. Cover the surrounding skin with Vaseline first to avoid irritation, and wear rubber gloves to squeeze out the latex. Within a few hours a slightly inflamed ring of skin will appear around the wart, which should gradually shrivel and drop off.

# FRUIT

*Apples, pears, and rhubarb*

*Stoned fruit*

*Citrus fruit*

*Berry fruit*

*Tropical fruit*

*Dried fruit*

# VEGETABLES

*Root vegetables*

*Soft vegetables*

*Onions, leeks, and garlic*

*Cruciferous vegetables*

*Salad vegetables*

*Edible seaweed*

*Fungi and Mediterranean vegetables*

# VEGETABLES

Vegetables have long been promoted for their protective role in the diet, against coronary heart disease, constipation, and, more recently, cancer. The huge range of vegetables—from humble root vegetables and brassicas, through salad vegetables to the more exotic Mediterranean types and edible seaweeds (not to mention the powerful **Allium** family of onions, leeks, and garlic)—is renowned for its vitamin and mineral content, and enjoying vegetables raw or lightly cooked is good insurance that their many protective constituents will be retained.

PAK CHOI

The World Cancer Research report released in 1998 provided considerable population-based evidence of the role of fruit and vegetable consumption in cancer prevention. And recent studies in Italy and other countries have provided strong evidence for protection against many forms of cancer, consistently linked to vegetable consumption, specifically of fresh or raw vegetables. Research has identified that carotenoids, vitamins C and E, selenium, dietary fiber, flavonoids, phenols, plant stenols, and protease inhibitors may be the substances in fruit and vegetables that exert these protective effects.

AVOCADO

Basing meals around generous quantities of vegetables has long been a tradition for some cultures; unfortunately, other cultures have viewed them chiefly as an accompaniment to meat or fish dishes. But with the increasing recognition of the value of vegetables, people are finding endless ways to incorporate them into meals to suit all palates: using raw or cooked vegetables on their own, combined in salads, soups, and stews, baked, puréed, and, increasingly, as interesting juices. Naturopaths and country remedies have long recommended vegetable juices for a wide range of conditions, including stomach ulcers, digestive complaints, and as a liver stimulant. Using vegetables in soups, stews, and purées ensures that any vitamins that have been leached into the cooking water are retained in the finished dish.

In many countries the potato and yam form the staple food, providing the main source of carbohydrate, along with some vitamins and minerals. However, when counting toward your "five portions a day," the potato moves into the starchy carbohydrate category and no longer counts as a vegetable.

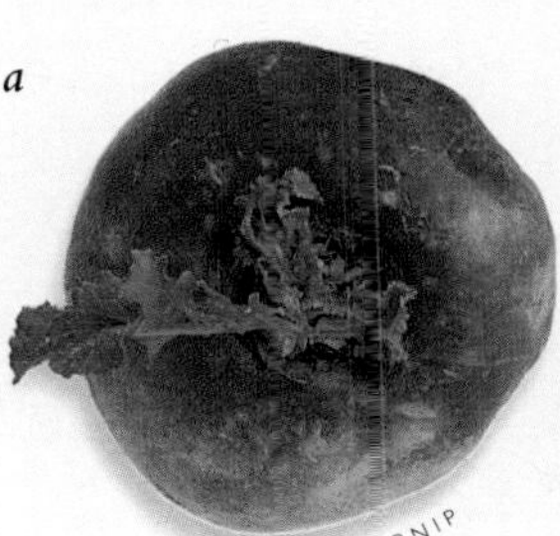

TURNIP

# ROOT VEGETABLES

*Prized for their vitamin and fiber content*

Many root vegetables, such as potatoes, yams, sweet potatoes, rutabagas, and carrots, are highly recommended for the healthy and filling starchy carbohydrate that they add to any diet. Unfortunately, those trying to lose weight are often mistakenly advised to avoid root vegetables, because they are thought to be high in calories. Actually it is the added sauces or fat that contribute the bulk of the calories. These humble, but important, vegetables are also good contributors of vitamins A, B, C, and E, small amounts of trace minerals, and a valuable source of dietary fiber—particularly if the skins are eaten.

FLORENCE FENNEL

Deep-red and yellow root vegetables, such as beets, carrots, sweet potatoes, and turnips, provide beneficial amounts of vitamin A, in addition to trace minerals. When they are in season, these are economical, flavorful, and filling foods. Less well-known or used root vegetables, like artichokes (both globe and Jerusalem), parsnips, and fennel, should also be given a recognized place in meals for their important contribution of vitamins and minerals.

RADISHES

Most root vegetables are served cooked—boiled, baked, mashed, or combined with other ingredients to make soups and stews—where they maintain a large proportion of their nutrients. Some, such as carrots, turnips, radishes, fresh baby globe artichokes, and fennel, when they are in season, can also be enjoyed raw.

# CARROTS

① ② ③ ④

*Energy per standard portion 21 calories*
*Rich in beta-carotene*

Carrots contain so much beta-carotene that a single carrot provides enough for your body to convert to a whole day's dose of vitamin A. This is vital for healthy skin and disease-resistant mucous membranes, which is why carrots are so important for the protection of the lungs and the function of the entire respiratory system. Vitamin A is also essential for proper night vision. Beta-carotene is much better absorbed from darker-colored, old cooked carrots—even more so if there is some fat or oil in the same meal to aid absorption—than baby new carrots. Whenever possible choose organically grown carrots, to avoid potentially high levels of pesticide residue.

In more than 40 published studies of the relationship between the occurrence of cancers and a high consumption of carrots, 75 percent of them revealed a definite reduction in cancer risk. As an anti aging food, carrots are believed to offer some protection against ultraviolet radiation, helping to protect the skin against damage and wrinkles.

Their other antioxidant vitamins, C and E, make them a must for anyone with arterial disease.

Traditional folklore has long advised the use of carrots in the treatment of diarrhea, particularly for small children and infants, for whom carrot purée is both a healthy food and good form of medicine. Naturopaths recommend a two-day fast on nothing but fresh carrot juice and plenty of mineral water to help stimulate the liver and relieve the symptoms of jaundice.

➕ *Valuable for cancer protection, the heart, circulation, and eyesight.*
➕ *Beneficial for the skin and mucous membranes.*
➕ *Best eaten old and cooked.*

POTATOES

OLD POTATOES
*Energy per 3¹/₂oz / 100g 75 calories*

FRENCH FRIES
*Energy per 3¹/₂oz / 100g 239 calories*
*Rich in fibre and vitamin C*

Potatoes are an extraordinary nutritional package and for generations they were the staple food of Irish agricultural workers. Potatoes supply fiber, B-complex vitamins, useful minerals, and enough vitamin C to keep scurvy at bay, even when boiled or baked. Baked potatoes are nutritionally superior, since many important nutrients, including potassium, are found in the skin.

For years doctors have crossed potatoes off the menu for would-be slimmers but, contrary to popular belief, they are in fact good news as part of a weight-loss regime. Not surprisingly, it is what you do to your potatoes that makes them healthy or otherwise. Roasting them in the bottom of the pan with your meat adds ¹/₈oz/5g of fat per 3¹/₂oz/100g of potatoes; homemade deep-fried french fries produce ¹/₂oz/15g of fat per 3¹/₂oz/100g. Potato chips provide almost 1¹/₂oz/36g of fat per 3¹/₂oz/100g (around ³/₄oz/26g for low-fat varieties!). Compare this with the

0.1g of fat per 3¹/₂oz/100g of boiled or baked potatoes, which are just as delicious.

Although its full nutritional value depends on the variety and the type of soil in which it is grown, the potato is in fact a better supplier of energy and protein than almost any other food crop. ▶

## SUPER FOOD

● Throughout northern and eastern Europe, naturopaths have used raw potato juice as a highly successful treatment for stomach ulcers and osteoarthritis. The treatment is simple—half a small glass of the raw juice, four times a day, for a month. The taste is vile, but you can camouflage it by adding apple and carrot juice, or even some honey. Alternatively, you can add the fresh juice to any soup just before you eat it, but not during cooking.

NEW POTATOES

**potatoes continued**

When cooked, potato starch is very easy to digest, making it suitable for invalids, anyone with digestive problems, and particularly as a weaning food for infants. The biological value of potato protein is just as good as that of the soybean, making it an ideal food for children, invalids, and vegetarians. It also provides more than one-third of the US recommended daily allowance of vitamin C (half of the UK).

- ✚ *Beneficial for digestive problems, chronic fatigue, and anemia.*
- ✚ *Best eaten baked in their skins, steamed, or boiled in minimal water.*
- ➖ *Potatoes that are damaged, have turned green, or are sprouting contain a toxic chemical called solanine, which may make you feel unwell, while larger quantities can be fatal.*

**FAST FOOD FACT**

● Potato-peel tea—containing high doses of potassium—is recommended in traditional medicine for high blood pressure.

## SWEET POTATOES
❶ ❸

*Energy per 3¹/₂oz / 100g 87 calories*
*Rich in starch and carotenoids*

The sweet potato is often confused with the yam (see *overleaf*), and many books describe them as alternative names for the same plant, but in fact they are separate species, with the yam being nutritionally inferior.

Sweet potatoes are an excellent source of starch, and therefore of energy. They provide some protein, vitamins C and E, and a huge amount of carotenoids, including beta-carotene. It is these and the other phytochemicals in the tubers that make sweet potatoes such a powerful anticancer food. A mere 3¹/₂oz/100g of sweet potato a day can dramatically reduce your risk of lung cancer. This is even more important if you are a smoker or ex-smoker.

- ✚ *Beneficial for visual problems and night vision.*
- ✚ *Good for skin problems and cancer protection.*
- ✚ *Best eaten boiled, mashed, or baked.*

## YAMS
❶ ❺ ❾

*Energy per 3¹/₂oz/100g 114 calories*
*Rich in carbohydrates*

Yams are extremely rich in carbohydrates and are used as a staple food, especially in Africa. They contain some protein and reasonable amounts of vitamin C, but virtually no vitamin A or E, and far less fiber than sweet potatoes. They are, however, a source of phytoestrogens and may help to protect against hormone-linked cancers, as well as assisting women who are going through the menopause.

Although a better source of energy than sweet potatoes, they contain slightly less protein, but this is believed to be of better nutritional quality. Ideally, eat plenty of both.

➕ *Good for energy.*
➕ *Best eaten boiled, baked, or mashed.*

## RUTABAGAS
❶ ❸

*Energy per 3¹/₂oz/100g 24 calories*
*Rich in vitamin C*

Another of the large and health-giving Cruciferae family, rutabaga is often thought of as no more than cattle fodder, but it is an excellent vegetable with a delicate flavor and all the anticancer properties of this group of plants. It contains significant amounts of vitamin C—3¹/₂oz/100g providing 50 percent of the US recommended daily allowance—useful amounts of vitamin A, almost no sodium, a little fiber and small amounts of trace minerals, depending on the soil quality. 3¹/₂oz/100g of rutabaga supplies only 24 calories and lots of filling bulk, making it a real bonus for the weight-watcher.

Mashed together with potato, rutabaga makes an excellent early weaning food for babies.

➕ *Good for cancer protection, skin problems, and weaning.*
➕ *Best eaten boiled or in stews, casseroles, and soups.*
➖ *Rutabagas contain goitrogens and they should therefore be eaten in moderation by anyone with thyroid problems or taking long-term thyroxine treatment.*

# BEETS

**❶ ❷ ❹ ❺ ❾**

*Energy per 100g/3¹/₂oz 36 calories*
*Rich in carotenoids and folate*

In Romany (Gypsy) medicine, beet juice was used as a blood-builder for patients who were pale and rundown. In Russia and eastern Europe it is used both to build up resistance and to treat convalescents after serious illness. The Swiss pioneer of organic horticulture, Dr. Hugo Brandenberger, developed a technique of lacto-fermentation to preserve organic beet juice in its most nutritious form to treat leukemia. Beets have for many years been used in the treatment of cancer in central Europe and now scientific research is beginning to explain their action. Specific anticarcinogens are bound to the red coloring matter, and beets also increase the cellular uptake of oxygen by as much as 400 percent.

Beet greens are equally valuable, containing beta-carotene and other carotenoids, lots of folate, potassium, some iron, and vitamin C. All of this makes the roots and greens excellent for women in general and especially for those planning pregnancy. Fresh juice made from raw beets makes a powerful blood-cleanser and tonic. It has also been valued for centuries as a digestive aid and liver stimulant.

✚ *Good for anemia and leukemia.*
✚ *Valuable for all the chronic fatigue syndromes and for convalescents.*
✚ *Beneficial for women of childbearing age; and beet leaves are especially good for osteoporosis.*
✚ *Best eaten raw and grated as a salad; the leaves boiled as a vegetable; baked in the oven, or as soup.*

## SUPER FOOD

● **An excellent treatment for postviral fatigue syndrome, TATT (Tired-All-The-Time syndrome), mononucleosis, or recovery from other debilitating illnesses is a mixture of beet, carrot, apple, and celery juice. Take a small wine glass of this delicious drink before each meal. But don't panic if it looks as though you are passing blood in your urine or stool—it's only the beets showing up!**

## PARSNIPS

❷ ❺

*Energy per 3¹/₂oz / 100g 64 calories*
*Rich in fiber, folic acid, and potassium*

This frequently ignored and much maligned vegetable deserves better treatment. It has a unique and delicious flavor and is worthy of more interesting applications than ending its life as a few cubes thrown into a stew.

The wild parsnip has long been known in most of Europe, where it grows on chalky soil along the roadsides and around the edge of cultivated fields. Parsnips, like carrots, have been cultivated since ancient times—the Roman emperor Tiberius had fresh parsnips brought all the way from the banks of the Rhine River to Rome. In Germany they are often eaten with salted fish during Lent; in Holland they are used to make soup; in Ireland they were boiled with water and hops in order to make beer; and in the English countryside tradition, they were even made into jam and parsnip wine.

The great herbalists Culpeper, Gerard, Tournefort, and even John Wesley, had nothing but good to say of parsnips as a highly nutritious food—for cattle and pigs, as well as humans. And they weren't wrong. The parsnip is a prime example of food that should be eaten when in season. The modern supermarket trend to have all foods available from the four corners of the earth throughout the year means that over-cultivated, forced, and artificially-fed produce ends up on the plate, often containing very little flavor and almost certainly diminished nutritional value.

Parsnips are a good source of healthy calories, fiber, potassium, folic acid, vitamin E, and traces of minerals and other B vitamins. They taste at their best and sweetest after the first hard frosts of winter.

✚ *Good for fatigue and constipation.*
✚ *Best eaten boiled, mashed, or roasted (in vegetable oil).*

## TURNIPS

① ⑥ ⑦

*Energy per 3½oz / 100g 23 calories*
*Rich in vitamin C and fiber*

Turnips are another member of the Cruciferae family, with all the healing properties of this amazing family of plants. Those who grow their own turnips know the delights of eating the green, leafy tops as a succulent early spring vegetable. These have long been used as a treatment for gout and arthritis in traditional medicine, because they eliminate uric acid from the body.

A thin purée of turnips, cooked in milk, is an old country remedy for bronchitis. And turnips are a good source of fiber, as well as containing small but useful amounts of calcium, phosphorus, potassium, and some B vitamins. They are also a good source of vitamin C.

➕ *Good for gout, arthritis, and chest infections.*
➕ *A useful cancer-protector.*
➕ *Best eaten raw in salads, lightly boiled, or added to soups and stews.*
➖ *Turnips contain goitrogens and they should therefore be eaten in moderation by anyone with thyroid problems or taking long-term thyroxine treatment.*

## FLORENCE FENNEL

② ⑧

*Energy per 100g / 3½oz 50 calories*
*Rich in volatile oils*

For more than 2,000 years varieties of fennel have been grown for the delicate flavor of their pale-green fronds, which go ideally with fish. The seeds have also been used medicinally for hundreds of years (see p.174). But the Florence fennel variety is grown as much for its large, greenish-white bulb, with its definite taste and distinctive smell of anise. It is the volatile oils, such as anisic acid, limonine, fenchone, and anethole, that impart its unique flavor as well as its medicinal properties. Although nutritionally not a powerhouse of vitamins and minerals, the fennel bulb is low in calories and helps to eliminate surplus fluids from the body.

➕ *Useful for digestive problems, especially excessive flatulence.*
➕ *A mild diuretic.*
➕ *Best eaten raw, braised, or boiled.*

### FAST FOOD FACT

● Add a few slices of fennel to any salad or pop some in your sandwiches for an extra boost.

JERUSALEM ARTICHOKE

GLOBE ARTICHOKE

## ARTICHOKES

② ④ ⑥ ⑧

GLOBE ARTICHOKES
*Energy per 3¹/₂oz / 100g 18 calories*
JERUSALEM ARTICHOKES
*Energy per 3¹/₂oz / 100g 41 calories*
*Rich in cynarine or potassium*

Every French housewife knows that the globe artichoke is a boon to the digestion and a powerful stimulant of the gall bladder and liver. Rich in a bitter chemical called cynarine, it traditionally forms the first course of any overrich meal because it stimulates the production of bile, which makes the digestion of fats much easier. Bile works in exactly the same way as dish-washing liquid on greasy dishes—it breaks the fat down into minute globules, thereby dramatically increasing the surface area that is exposed to the stomach's digestive juices.

Herbalists have traditionally used extracts of the artichoke to treat high blood pressure, and it is also known to help the body get rid of cholesterol. Together with its diuretic properties, the artichoke is a cleanser and detoxifier, which makes it useful for people suffering from gout, arthritis, or rheumatism.

If you're lucky enough to find fresh baby artichokes, eat them raw with a little olive oil for maximum healing benefits, or lightly sautéed with pasta.

The globe artichoke is a type of thistle, originating from the Mediterranean part of Europe. It is not to be confused with the Jerusalem artichoke, a North American plant that found its way to France during the 1600s and is rich in potassium, but not much else. Both types, however, contain a chemical called inulin, instead of starch. Like fiber, inulin does not get broken down during digestion but is fermented by the action of bacteria in the large bowel (colon), so it can be an embarrassing source of flatulence. Jerusalem artichokes are best eaten as soup.

➕ *Good for liver and gall-bladder problems, gout, arthritis, and rheumatism.*

➕ *Help to lower cholesterol and have a good diuretic effect.*

➕ *Best eaten raw, if very small; large globe artichokes should be boiled and eaten hot or cold.*

## RADISHES

❶ ❷ ❼

*Energy per standard portion 1 calorie*
*Rich in potassium and sulfur*

The ancient Pharaohs cultivated radishes and thought them a valuable food source—so much so that workers building the pyramids were paid in garlic, onions, and radishes. And in traditional Chinese medicine radishes were listed in the medical texts toward the middle of the seventh century. Although originally native to southern Asia, they are now widely cultivated throughout Europe, Britain, China, and Japan, although they did not reach Britain until the mid-1500s, appearing in an early herbal in 1597.

Radishes are part of the Cruciferae family and as such contain glucosilinates and other sulfurous compounds, which are valuable for those at risk from cancer. But it is for gall-bladder and liver problems that the herbalists have found this delicious vegetable most useful. Radish juice acts powerfully on the gall bladder, stimulating the discharge of bile, as French studies have demonstrated.

Radishes contain many other nutritional goodies as well—plenty of potassium, a little calcium, lots of sulfur, a reasonable amount of vitamin C, and some folic acid and selenium. But an excess of the hot, stinging radish can be too much of a good thing, irritating rather than stimulating the liver, kidneys, and gall bladder.

Radishes should be eaten as fresh as possible, while still young and crisp—their tops should be eaten at the same time, aiding their digestion.

➕ *Good for cancer protection.*
➕ *Beneficial for liver and gall-bladder problems, for indigestion, and for chest problems.*
➕ *Best eaten raw.*
➖ *Radishes should not be eaten by those with ulcers, gastric inflammation, or thyroid problems.*

# SOFT VEGETABLES

*Prized for their vitamin,*
*beta-carotene, and fiber content*

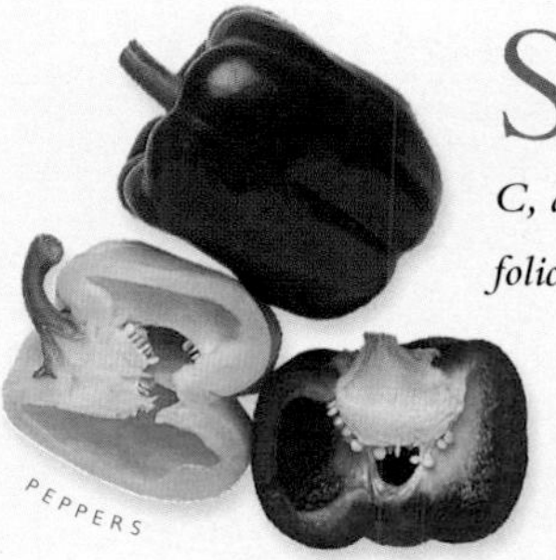

*S*oft vegetables are good suppliers of the valuable antioxidant nutrients A, C, and E, beta-carotene, small amounts of folic acid, and are a reasonable source of dietary fiber.

*PEPPERS*

With its smooth, oily taste provided by monounsaturated fatty acids, the avocado is unique as a vegetable. Though often thought to be high in calories, these few extra calories provide antioxidants that are helpful in the prevention of cancer and coronary heart disease.

Both avocados and peppers are best eaten raw. Zucchini can be eaten raw or lightly sautéed, while squash—which is not high in nutritional value or flavor—makes a pleasant, low-calorie option when it is either baked or stuffed with other vegetables.

Pumpkin and sweetcorn are much more widely used in Africa, the Caribbean, and North America than they are in Europe. When cooked and eaten immediately after picking, corn on the cob is truly a feast of sweet flavor and high nutrient value; the canned version is a healthy choice for fiber, if you watch out for the amount of added salt. Pumpkin is gradually becoming more widely used in Europe for its versatility in soups, stews, and sweet pies; it provides an excellent source of beta-carotene.

*SWEETCORN*

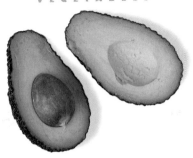

## AVOCADOS

**❶ ❸ ❹ ❺ ❾**

*Energy per standard portion 276 calories*
*Rich in potassium and vitamin E*

Avocados probably started life in Peru, where it is believed they were originally cultivated 8,000–9,000 years ago. In Guatemala the fruit, dried leaves, fresh leaves, rind, bark, and even the seed are used medicinally by the indigenous natives.

The avocado is rich in potassium, lack of which can lead to depression and exhaustion. It also contains vitamin B₆, which helps iron out the mood-swings in women suffering from premenstrual syndrome. Thanks to their vitamin E and B content, avocados also aid in the relief of stress and sexual problems such as infertility and impotence.

Every slimmer thinks that avocados are fattening, but calorie for calorie they offer super nutritional value. Their high content of mono-unsaturated fats—especially oleic acid, like olive oil—makes them one of the most powerful antioxidant foods. It is this particular property that offers protection against heart disease, strokes, and cancer.

The avocado's flesh and oil have long been popular with traditional practitioners as a skin treatment and it is now known that chemicals in the avocado stimulate the production of collagen, which helps to smooth out wrinkles and give skin that wonderful young fresh look—cheaper and safer than either injections or dermabrasion. It is also a good source of vitamins A and E, which are excellent for the skin, whether the avocado is eaten or pulverized and used as a face mask.

Because the fats in avocado are easily digestible and it contains anti-fungal and antibacterial chemicals too, puréed avocado is an excellent food for invalids, convalescents, and sick children. Guacamole is not just something you eat with tacos, but a high-protein, high-energy, high-protection-factor food.

➕ *Good for the heart, circulation, and the skin.*
➕ *Help in the relief of PMS.*
➕ *Cancer-protective.*
➕ *Best eaten raw and ripe.*

## PEPPERS

**❶ ❸ ❹**

*Energy per standard portion 2–3 calories*
*Rich in vitamins A and C*

Sweet peppers, together with pimento and chili peppers, are all members of the Capsicum genus and belong to the Solanaceae family, which also includes potatoes, eggplants, and tomatoes. Sweet peppers are green, and as they ripen they become red or yellow. The entire Capsicum family was native to the Americas and it was Columbus who introduced them to Europe, from where they soon spread to Africa and Asia. Native North Americans have used peppers for over 5,000 years as both food and medicine *(see Cayenne on p.179)*.

Sweet peppers are an important source of vital nutrients. They are low in calories (15–32 per 3½oz/100g), very rich in vitamin C (120–40mg per 3½oz/100g), and an important source of vitamin A, particularly red peppers—3½oz/100g of which provide almost a whole day's requirements. They also supply useful amounts of folic acid, some fiber, and potassium. Because of the waxy chemicals in the skin of sweet peppers, they are protected against oxidation and their vitamin C content remains high, even some weeks after harvesting, especially if they are kept in a refrigerator. Also nutritionally important are the bioflavonoids in peppers, which are valuable for their powerful antioxidant properties. This makes peppers protective against heart and circulatory disease, as well as some forms of cancer.

✛ *Good for skin problems and the mucous membranes.*
✛ *Beneficial for night and color vision.*
✛ *Useful for natural resistance.*
✛ *Best eaten raw or char-broiled.*

### SUPER FOOD

● Peppers are a significant source of other carotenoids, as well as beta-carotene, most important lutein and zeaxanthin, both of which are protective against age-related macular degeneration (AMD), which is the most important cause of visual impairment in the elderly.

## SWEETCORN

②

*Energy per 3¹/₂oz / 100g 54 calories*
*Rich in fiber and protein*

Sweetcorn, or corn on the cob, is a variety of maize bred for eating as a vegetable, rather than conversion into flour or meal. These sweetcorn hybrids are designed to slow down the conversion of sugar to starch, both during the ripening process and after harvesting, and taste much sweeter than maize, although the sweetest corn on the cob is one picked from your garden, cooked and eaten within the hour. Canned sweetcorn contains only one-third of the starch, and five times as much natural sugar as fresh sweetcorn. But beware—it contains a great deal of salt, whereas a fresh cob contains virtually none.

Sweetcorn is a good source of protein and also contains significant amounts of fiber, some vitamins A and E, and small amounts of the B vitamins, including folic acid.

➕ *Good for vegetarian diets, for providing energy and fiber.*
➕ *Best eaten boiled whole or as separate grains, especially in salads.*

## PUMPKINS

❶ ❸ ❼

*Energy per standard portion 11 calories*
*Rich in beta-carotene*

Pumpkins are full of beta-carotene, the vitamin A precursor that helps protect against cancer, heart troubles, and respiratory disease. In population studies, people eating plenty of pumpkin ran a lower risk of getting lung cancer. And because of their vitamin A content, pumpkins are also a useful food for vegetarians. The seeds are a very good source of protein and zinc *(see p.105).*

➕ *Good for cancer protection.*
➕ *Useful for breathing problems.*
➕ *Best eaten cooked as a vegetable, sweet as a pie, or as soup.*

### FAST FOOD FACT

● To treat tapeworm, take 2oz/60g of fresh pumpkin seeds, remove the outer skins by scalding them and grind the green pulp to a paste with a little milk. Take after fasting for 12 hours, and two hours later take four teaspoons of castor oil mixed with some fruit juice. Wait for the tapeworm to be passed, usually within three hours. Do not use castor oil for any other reason.

ZUCCHINI

## ZUCCHINI AND SQUASH

❸

ZUCCHINI
*Energy per standard portion 18 calories*

SQUASH
*Energy per standard portion 12 calories*
*Rich in folic acid and potassium*

Zucchini and squash belong to the same family as melons, pumpkins, and cucumbers. Zucchini are more nutritious than squash because the skin, which is rich in beta-carotene, can be eaten. This delicious and versatile vegetable is not a baby squash but a specific variety of its own, although left to grow it will end up looking like a squash. Squash has very little flavor and even less nutritional value, but it can be a healthy way of presenting other foods—stuffed, baked, or steamed.

You can serve zucchini flowers raw in salads or, for a delicious treat, fill them with ricotta cheese, dip them in batter and deep-fry for one minute. Use olive oil or pure sun- or safflower oil—the taste is delicious and the extra calories worth it for the occasional pleasure.

For a cheap and instant vitamin A boost, lightly cook some pasta, add two or three grated zucchini, some extra-virgin olive oil, black pepper, and fresh parsley. Sprinkle on some cheese and mix together well; accompany with a glass of red wine and fresh tomato and basil salad.

Zucchini and squash also contain folic acid—3½oz/100g supplying more than a quarter of our daily need—and are a rich source of potassium while being low in calories.

- ✚ *Good for slimmers.*
- ✚ *Zucchini are beneficial for skin problems.*
- ✚ *Zucchini are best eaten raw or slightly steamed, but with the skin on; squash, steamed or stuffed, then baked in the oven.*

### FAST FOOD FACT

● If your suffer from blackheads or similar skin problems, a slice or two of squash or zucchini gently rubbed over the affected area will help to combat these stubborn spots by drying out the skin and blotting up any excess oils.

# ONIONS, LEEKS, AND GARLIC

*Prized for their sulfur compounds*

All three vegetables in this group were traditionally advocated by the Native North Americans, the Romans, and the ancient Egyptians as remedies for various ills, ranging from colds, bronchitis, and throat problems to arthritis and gout. Many of these remedies are still valid today; and extensive recent research has also looked at the role of these plants in the prevention of cancer and coronary heart disease.

GARLIC

Onions, leeks, and garlic are all plants from the Allium *genus* and are a major source of sulfur compounds. One of these compounds, allicin, is released when the vegetable is cut or crushed and causes their characteristic smell and flavor, as well as encouraging the elimination of cholesterol from the body. Onions contain less allicin than garlic, but do contain significant concentrations of antioxidant flavonoids, this being one of the subjects of interest in studying their potential influence on cancer and coronary heart disease. Evidence from population studies as well as clinical trials has now prompted governments to recognize the protective effect of both garlic and onions against these particular diseases.

ONION

Though these vegetables are all low in calories, they are not high in nutritional value. It is worth noting, however, that the green parts of both scallions and leeks supply small quantities of vitamins, minerals, and fiber.

## ONIONS

④ ⑥ ⑦ ⑧

*Energy per standard portion 22 calories*
*Rich in vitamin C*

Onions are impressive country medicine for a huge range of ailments—among them anemia, bronchitis and asthma, genitourinary infections, arthritis and rheumatism, gout, and premature aging.

Originally natives of the northern hemisphere, they have been cultivated for many thousands of years, as much for their medicinal value as for their flavor. In medieval times they were hung in bunches on door posts as a protection against the plague. The wild onion is a traditional medicine of the Native North Americans, who use them in the treatment of colds and to soothe insect stings.

Onions star in hundreds of old wives' remedies, most deliciously as the famous onion soup that is consumed at the end of a night on the tiles, which is part of Parisian mythology. And traditional Chinese herbalists use scallions as a poultice to treat boils and as a medicine to relieve nasal congestion. Onion is even reputed to be both an aphrodisiac and a remedy that stimulates the growth of new hair.

Onions contain the enzyme allinase, which is released when you slice the bulb. The action of allinase on sulfur compounds results in the chemicals that not only give onions their flavor but also make you cry. Onions are extremely low in calories, but scallions, or green onions, are a good source of vitamin C, as well as small amounts of some B vitamins and traces of minerals. ▶

RED ONION

SCALLIONS

**onions continued**

Onions belong to the same family as garlic, leeks, scallions, chives and shallots—and, like garlic, they are currently the subject of extensive medical research. Science now confirms the age-old reputation of the onion as a cure-all, especially their protective action on the circulatory system. In a trial carried out at the Royal Victoria Infirmary in Britain, the blood samples of volunteers who ate no onions with a fatty fried breakfast of bacon and eggs showed an increased tendency to clot—a state that could eventually lead to life-threatening thrombosis. The blood of those who ate fried onions with their bacon and eggs showed a reduced tendency to clot. The results speak for themselves. In a similar study that was conducted in India, rich fatty food pushed up the levels of blood cholesterol—and onions pulled them right back down.

Furthermore, Dr. Victor Gurewitch of Tufts University, Massachusetts, has found that eating just half a raw onion daily raises blood levels of beneficial high-density lipoproteins (HDLs) by an average of 30 percent. In other trials onions were found to be highly effective against asthma and in lowering blood-sugar levels.

Onions are also powerfully diuretic, dissolving and eliminating urea, thus making them useful in the treatment of rheumatism, arthritis, and gout. Their traditional value in the treatment of chest infections is due to their powerful antibacterial activity.

➕ *Good for reducing cholesterol and preventing blood clots.*

➕ *Useful for bronchitis, asthma, arthritis, gout, respiratory problems, and chilblains.*

➕ *Best eaten raw, baked in their skins, or in traditional recipes like onion soup.*

### FAST FOOD FACTS

● For colic in babies, slice an onion, infuse it in hot water for a few minutes, allow to cool, then give the baby a teaspoonful.

● For the treatment of chilblains, rub the affected area with slices of raw onion.

● To reduce a moderately high temperature, bake a large onion in a hot oven for 40 minutes, then crush to extract the juice, which should be mixed with an equal amount of honey. Take two teaspoons of the mixture every two to three hours until the temperature falls.

## LEEKS

**1 4 6 7 8**

*Energy per standard portion 18 calories*
*Rich in beta-carotene and potassium*

Leeks have 4,000 years of history as both food and medicine. One writer described pre-biblical Egypt as a country in which "onions are adored and leeks are gods."

The Greeks and Romans held leeks in the highest esteem, especially for the treatment of throat and voice problems. The infamous Emperor Nero ate leeks every day to improve the quality of his singing voice.

And this vegetable became the national emblem of the Welsh after the historic triumph of their King Cadwaller, when the Welsh defeated the Saxons in A.D. 690; during the conflict the Celtic soldiers wore leeks so that they could recognize friend from foe.

Leeks are a member of the all-powerful *Allium* family—garlic, onions, chives—and, though not as rich in the anticarcinogenic chemicals, they too are important in the detoxification process. They are also antibacterial and, as such, contribute to protecting against stomach cancer, destroying some of the bacteria in the gut that change harmless nitrates into cancer-causing nitrites.

When preparing leeks, most people discard the dark-green leafy parts that normally grow above ground, and eat only the white stem. This is a great mistake because the green bits are a good source of beta-carotene, which the body converts into vitamin A.

Although leeks contain only small amounts of vitamins, minerals, and fiber, they are a reasonable source of folic acid and vitamin C and a good source of potassium. They are diuretic and have the ability to eliminate uric acid, so they make an excellent food for anyone who may be suffering from gout or arthritis.

✚ *Beneficial for all chest and voice problems and for sore throats.*

✚ *Useful for reducing high blood pressure and cholesterol levels, and for cancer protection.*

✚ *Good for gout and arthritis.*

✚ *Best eaten lightly steamed, hot or cold with a vinaigrette dressing.*

GARLIC BULB

# GARLIC

❶ ❷ ❸ ❹ ❺ ❼ ❽

*Energy per standard portion 3 calories*
*Rich in ailicin*

The first herb planted by Roman doctors on arriving in a new country was garlic, even then the most valued of medicinal herbs. It was brought to Britain by Roman centurions, who wedged pieces of fresh garlic between their toes to prevent the inevitable fungal infections that resulted from their long, arduous marches. From ancient Egypt through the civilizations of ancient Greece and Rome, England in the Middle Ages to the end of the nineteenth century, garlic was the most widely used medicinal plant in the world. It has long been known that garlic has a broad antibacterial effect—first proved scientifically by Louis Pasteur in 1858. It can destroy fungal infections and is a useful antidote to some poisons, especially alcohol and heavy metals.

A few years ago, within the space of one week, three separate patients told me that their doctors were puzzled by changes in the behavior of their blood samples. They had all consulted me for different reasons, but all had heart or circulatory problems and were taking anticoagulant drugs to "thin" their blood—and all had had their doses of medication reduced. Why did I find this news so exciting? Because the only treatment that I had prescribed that was identical for all of them was large doses of garlic.

The latest research into the powerful effect of garlic on the heart and circulation shows that it has the unique ability both to prevent and ▶

## FAST FOOD FACTS

● As a home remedy, try a crushed clove mixed with two teaspoons of honey, and a squeeze of lemon juice dissolved in a cup of hot water. Take three times a day, for catarrh, bronchitis, and sinus problems.

● For indigestion, constipation, and mild stomach upsets, crush a clove of garlic into a cup of warm milk and drink after meals.

● And if you suffer from cystitis or other urinary infections, crush a clove into a small carton of natural yogurt and make sure that you eat one pot each morning and evening.

GARLIC CLOVES

**garlic continued**

treat some of the factors that are linked to heart disease. Scientists who study the distribution of illnesses in different populations know that in those countries where large quantities of garlic are eaten there is a lower rate of death from heart attacks despite the fact that in many of these countries there is just as much smoking and drinking as there is in Britain. Britain has the lowest consumption of garlic in Europe and the highest rate of premature death from heart disease; however, heart disease has declined considerably in the United States, following a successful health-education campaign mounted by the government.

The sulfur compound, allicin, which is released when garlic is crushed, both encourages the elimination of cholesterol from the body and reduces the quantity of unhealthy fats produced by the liver. In healthy volunteers on fatty diets it has been shown to reduce the level of cholesterol in the blood by up to 15 percent. At a recent International Garlic Symposium in Berlin some of the most exciting work concerned the reduction of blood cholesterol, high blood pressure, and blood clots, the three most important factors

involved in heart disease and strokes. In a study of patients with raised cholesterol, half were given a placebo and half garlic, in the form of standardized tablets (no dietary advice was included). After 16 weeks the placebo group remained the same but in the garlic-eating group cholesterol levels went down by an average of 12 percent.

A report in the *British Medical Journal* confirms the benefits of garlic in heart disease, but emphasizes the importance of using preparations containing adequate amounts of the active substance, allicin, which may not be present in extracts or oils made by steam distillation. Meanwhile, work in the eye hospital at Aachen University, in the Transfusion Institute at the University of Saarland and at the University of Munich has provided clear evidence that garlic dilates the blood vessels and reduces the stickiness of blood.

Garlic also has cancer-protective properties. Professor Kourounakis from Greece and Professor Wargovich from the University of Texas are both working in this field. The Greeks have investigated the way in which garlic can destroy the highly destructive chemicals known as free radicals, which can initiate the ▶

GARLIC CAPSULES

**garlic continued**

production of cancerous cells. Wargovich is investigating a wide range of natural compounds and studying their protective effect against cancer. Both before and after exposure to the toxic compounds, garlic reduced and, in some cases, prevented the development of some artificially induced cancers in laboratory tests.

✚ *Good for cancer protection, lowering cholesterol levels, reducing blood pressure, and improving circulation.*

✚ *Beneficial for coughs, bronchitis, catarrh, sore throats, asthma, indigestion, constipation, diarrhea, and stomach upsets.*

✚ *Useful for fungal infections such as athlete's foot.*

✚ *Best eaten raw in salads, baked whole in the oven or, if fried, not allowed to go brown.*

## SUPER FOOD

● So what is the best way to eat this powerful bulb, which can help bronchitis, catarrh, sore throats, asthma, indigestion, constipation, diarrhea, and even athlete's foot? The quality varies, depending on the soil in which the garlic is grown. The best is grown organically in China, the United States, and southern France and gives a rich yield of the allicin compound, which is released by crushing but may be destroyed by cooking at high temperatures, especially frying.

● If you don't fancy munching a raw garlic clove each day, you can take a garlic supplement. Look for whole, dried garlic powder in tablets, which retain the goodness of the fresh clove. There must be a high proportion of allicin and the product should be standardized—each pill in each batch containing an exact dose, equivalent to a medium, fresh, high-quality clove.

# CRUCIFEROUS VEGETABLES

*Prized for their vitamin C
and beta-carotene content*

This large group of vegetables of the cruciferous family and Brassica *genus* is widely grown, but has been sadly overlooked for its contribution to nutrition. This is partly because these vegetables are often badly prepared, making them unpalatable and losing both flavor and valuable nutrients.

SAVOY CABBAGE

The possible protective effect of the cruciferous family has been widely researched, and there is now convincing evidence of its protective powers against many cancers, including colon, stomach, and oral cancers. Anticarcinogenic indoles—compounds formed from glucosinolates in cruciferous vegetables—have been shown to be protective against breast cancer, via their effect on estrogen metabolism. The report "Food, Nutrition and the Prevention of Cancer: A Global Perspective," published in 1998 by the World Cancer Research Fund, provides an assessment of many of these studies.

Brassicas are generally good sources of vitamin A, beta-carotene, folic acid, vitamin C, potassium, and fiber, and many are used for their potential medicinal properties. These all add up to good reasons for including a wide variety of these vegetables in your daily diet. Many are delicious raw; if lightly cooked in their own juices, as part of a stir-fry or soup, they provide economical and interesting ways of increasing your nutrient intake and helping to protect against disease.

SAUERKRAUT

## BROCCOLI

**①③④⑤⑥⑨**

*Energy per 3¹/₂oz / 100g 33 calories*
*Rich in beta-carotene*

Ever since the scare over President Reagan's bowel cancer, broccoli has rapidly become a four-star vegetable. The American National Cancer Institute advised a special diet for the President, including eating copious amounts of broccoli.

Like other members of the cruciferous family of vegetables, broccoli has been shown to have protective powers against cancer. According to an analysis made at the National Cancer Institute in 1987, six out of seven major population studies showed that the more cruciferous vegetables you eat, the lower your chances of developing cancer of the colon, while other cancers appear to slow down as well.

In response to cell damage, the major glucosinolates in cruciferous vegetables are converted into indoles—nitrogen components that may offer some protection against cancer. In Japan, where the incidence of colon cancer is extremely low, the average intake of glucosinolates is 100mg a day. In Britain, where there is a high incidence of colon cancer, it is less than a quarter of this amount.

Broccoli is also rich in carotenoids, including the vitamin A precursor beta-carotene, which is known to inhibit the activation of cancer cells. It is the presence of these carotenoids that make broccoli such a favorite in the treatment of skin problems.

The combined presence of iron, vitamin C, and folate also helps with the improvement of anemia, protects against birth defects and raises energy levels in the chronically fatigued.

Since 3¹/₂oz/100g of broccoli provides almost one-third of the daily requirement of vitamin E, this vegetable is equally at home as a guardian of good heart health and circulatory efficiency. Compounds produced during the digestion of cruciferous vegetables also suppress free-radical formation, making crucifers valuable for those with joint problems.

✚ *Good for chronic fatigue syndrome, anemia, stress, and women planning pregnancy.*
✚ *Valuable for cancer protection.*
✚ *Useful for skin problems, recurrent infections, and lowered immunity.*
✚ *Best eaten very lightly steamed.*

**75**

SAVOY CABBAGE

## CABBAGE

① ② ③ ⑤ ⑦ ⑨

RED CABBAGE
*Energy per standard portion 19 calories*

WHITE CABBAGE
*Energy per standard portion 24 calories*
*Rich in iron, folate, vitamin C, and beta-carotene*

Cabbage has rightfully earned its reputation as "the medicine of the poor." The ancient Romans valued it; herbalists in the Middle Ages also used it; and nineteenth- and early twentieth-century Europeans cooked cabbage, juiced it, and made poultices out of it. But recent methods of cooking have tended to ruin this king of vegetables.

Cabbage contains healing mucilaginous substances, which are similar to those produced by the mucous membrane of the gut and stomach for their own protection.

Traditionally European naturopaths have used it to treat stomach ulcers, prescribing 5 cups/1l of fresh cabbage juice to be taken daily, in divided doses, for ten days. Modern research has shown that this regime results in complete healing.

Cabbage is also rich in sulfur compounds—these are what cause the smell of overcooked cabbage—making it valuable for chest infections and for skin complaints.

Dark-green leafy cabbage is rich in iron and its high content of vitamin C makes for better absorption by the body. It should be eaten in abundance by anyone suffering from anemia and by all women of child-bearing age, especially because it is extremely rich in folate. It is also an excellent source of beta-carotene, another aid to healthy skin.

By far the most exciting development in the history of cabbage is the discovery of its enormous cancer-protecting value. Population studies have shown that ▶

RED CABBAGE

WHITE CABBAGE

**cabbage continued**

where people eat large quantities of cabbage (and its relatives), some cancers—particularly cancer of the lung, colon, breast, and uterus—are far less common. As soon as brassica leaves are chopped, crushed, juiced, or cooked, enzymes are released in the plant, which convert its glucosinolates into anticarcinogenic indoles.

Overcooking cabbage in boiling water not only leads to major nutrient losses into the water, but also to the disappearance or deactivation of many of its healing compounds. Cooked cabbage may also be indigestible, so steam or boil it in its own juices, in a sealed pan, for as short a time as possible. The majority of the nutrients are found in the dark outer leaves, so make sure you do not discard them.

Surprisingly, animal studies have also shown that cabbage can have a mild protective effect against radiation, which may be useful for those working with VDU screens, having radiation treatment or lots of X-rays. Centuries of use have also given the cabbage a traditional role as a vegetable stress-buster.

➕ *Useful for stomach ulcers.*

➕ *Good for anemia, respiratory diseases, and acne.*

➕ *Best eaten raw, slightly steamed, or boiled in minimal water.*

➖ *People with sensitive skins should be careful when handling brassicas, which can cause contact dermatitis.*

➖ *All brassicas should be eaten in moderation by anyone taking the thyroid medication thyroxine, or iodine for an underactive thyroid.*

## FAST FOOD FACT

● Cabbage can be used as a poultice for arthritic joints. Remove two or three of the largest outer leaves. Cut out the stalks and the central veins and bruise the leaves all over with a rolling pin or knife handle. Wrap them around a hot-water pipe, steam them for a few minutes, or put them in a microwave until they are comfortably warm—but not scalding hot. Wrap the leaves around the affected joint and secure in place with a crêpe bandage or thin towel. Leave for 15 minutes and repeat several times a day. This treatment is great for osteoarthritis, rheumatoid arthritis, sports injuries, strains, and sprains.

## SAUERKRAUT

**❶ ❷ ❸ ❻**

*Energy per standard portion 3 calories*
*Rich in vitamin C*

Sauerkraut is an ingenious method of preserving cabbage. While still raw, the cabbage is finely shredded and layered in a stone crock, with sea salt and spices such as juniper berries. Each layer is pressed firmly down. By the time the crock is full, the cabbage juices have fermented to produce that soured taste, which you either love or loathe. Large-scale commercial production is done in oak barrels or stainless-steel vats.

For many centuries sauerkraut was a dietary staple of the poor peasantry all over Europe, a good way of preserving the fall glut of cabbages so that they could go on being eaten through the lean months of winter. It can truly be called a wonder-food, since the enzymes and vitamin C of the cabbage are well preserved, and it must have saved millions from death or debility due to scurvy. It was sauerkraut that made possible the long voyages of Captain Cook and the astonishing empire-building feats of the Dutch during the seventeenth century. The Dutch merchant ships were well supplied with sauerkraut for their long voyages to the Far East and the Americas, while the crews of Holland's commercial rivals at sea were dying of scurvy.

In addition to its vitamin C content—3½oz/100g supplying one-sixth of the US recommended daily allowance—sauerkraut also contains calcium and potassium. Traditionally used as much for medicine as for food, sauerkraut is useful for the relief of indigestion, stomach ulcers, skin problems, arthritis, and colds.

The lactic acid that forms in the cabbage during the long process of fermentation does a wonderful clean-up job in the digestive tract. This allows the beneficial gut bacteria to multiply, kill off the harmful bacteria and produce a healthy, well-functioning digestive tract.

➕ *Good for cancer protection and for boosting immunity.*
➕ *Beneficial for digestive problems.*
➕ *Best eaten pickled, though it can be heated.*

## KOHLRABI

② ③ ④ ⑦

*Energy per 3¹/₂oz / 100g 23 calories*
*Rich in potassium, folic acid, and*
*vitamin C*

Sometimes called the turnip cabbage, kohlrabi is similar in taste to turnip. Although it is a cruciferous vegetable—a descendant of the original wild cabbage—it arrived in Germany from Italy in the mid-1500s. Kohlrabi is most popular in Germany, though health-conscious folk in other parts of the world have always valued this interesting member of the brassica family.

The food value and health benefits of kohlrabi are almost identical to those of cabbage. It is rich in potassium, a very good source of folic acid and vitamin C, but does not contain any beta-carotene.

➕ *Beneficial for anemia, respiratory diseases, and acne.*
➕ *Good for stomach ulcers.*
➕ *Best eaten raw, slightly steamed, or boiled in minimal water.*

## BRUSSELS SPROUTS

① ② ③ ④ ⑨

*Energy per 3¹/₂oz / 100g 42 calories*
*Rich in vitamin C and beta-carotene*

Brussels sprouts have most of the same health benefits as other brassicas. They are particularly rich in glucosinolates, one of the powerful anticancer chemicals (see *Cabbage on p.76*). Their high vitamin C content also helps to promote improved natural resistance to disease.

Sprouts are also a very good source of beta-carotene, which is a great aid to all skin problems. Their high fiber content makes them a good remedy for constipation and useful in the treatment of raised cholesterol and high blood pressure. And 3¹/₂oz/100g of sprouts provides more than half the daily requirement of folate, making them great food for women planning pregnancy.

Sprouts can cause flatulence, but this may be lessened by adding a few caraway or dill seeds when cooking.

➕ *Good for cancer protection and improved general resistance.*
➕ *Useful for skin problems and for constipation.*
➕ *Best eaten steamed.*
➖ *If you have thyroid problems, eat in modest amounts only.*

## SPINACH

❶ ❸ ❺ ❾

*Energy per standard portion 23 calories*
*Rich in chlorophyll and folic acid*

As every Popeye fan knows, spinach is rich in iron. Unfortunately, in this respect, generations of mothers who have tried forcing spinach down their children's throats have largely been wasting their time. The large amounts of iron and calcium in spinach are not easily available to the body, since spinach has high levels of oxalic acid. These combine with the minerals and are then excreted as insoluble salts.

But spinach is also very rich in the dark-green plant "blood" chlorophyll, so anemia patients, or those suffering from fatigue and mental strain, should eat plenty of it, preferably raw in salads. It is also exceptionally rich in folic acid, which is easily absorbed, 3½oz/100g providing three-quarters of the daily need. This should put spinach firmly on the shopping list of any woman who is either planning pregnancy or who is already expecting a baby.

Cancer patients, or those at risk from cancer, such as heavy smokers, should include plenty of spinach in their diet. Cancer research is increasingly focusing on the whole spectrum of carotenoids—not just beta-carotene—contained in dark-green or brightly colored fruit and vegetables, and spinach is even more highly endowed with these than carrots. In population studies, dark-green vegetables, with spinach heading the list, were found to be strongly protective against cancer.

➕ *Good for cancer protection and sight protection.*

➕ *Beneficial for pregnant women.*

➕ *Best eaten raw or cooked in the minutest possible amount of water.*

➖ *Spinach contains considerable uric acid, so it is best avoided by those with gout and arthritis.*

### SUPER FOOD

● One of the great unknown virtues of spinach is its ability to protect against the eye disease AMD (age-related macular degeneration). Scientists suggest that this is not due to its beta-carotene content but to two other compounds, known as lutein and zeaxanthin.

KALE

## COLLARD GREENS
### ❶

*Energy per 3¹/₂oz/100g 26 calories*
*Rich in phytochemicals*

More popular in the United States than in Europe, collard greens are another variety of these great health-promoting foods, rich in anticancer phytochemicals.

Like other Cruciferae, collard greens are rich in the indoles that specifically protect against hormone-mediated cancer; breast, ovary, prostate, and testicular cancer.

➕ *Useful for cancer protection.*
➕ *Best eaten lightly steamed.*

## KALE
### ❶

*Energy per 3¹/₂oz/100g 33 calories*
*Rich in beta-carotene*

Another brassica that is a member of the Cruciferae family, kale is grown specifically for its shoots and yellow leaves. It almost certainly started life like other varieties of its family in western Europe, particularly in the eastern Mediterranean area, but is now distributed throughout the world.

With all the anticancer properties of the brassica family and a huge amount of beta-carotene—3¹/₂oz/100g provides almost a whole day's dose for the average woman—kale deserves to be more popular. It has the advantage of being extremely hardy and can survive winter temperatures down to 5°F/-15°C, but can also cope with high temperatures during the summer.

One of the great traditional dishes of the hardy Dutch is *stampot*, a delicious combination of mashed potato mixed with lightly steamed, chopped kale.

➕ *Beneficial for cancer protection and general immunity.*
➕ *Best eaten lightly steamed.*

## PAK CHOI
❶

*Energy 3¹/₂oz / 100g 12 calories*
*Rich in folic acid, beta-carotene, and*
*vitamin C*

One of the most famous of all
the Oriental brassicas, pak choi
is the general name for several
members of this group. According to
historical accounts, the Chinese have
been cultivating these vegetables for
both food and medicine since the fifth
century. The Chinese cabbage is the
most important and the most widely
grown vegetable throughout eastern
Asia, Korea, and Taiwan.

Pak choi is an extremely nutritious
vegetable, providing potassium,
calcium, beta-carotene, folic acid, and
vitamin C, as well as small amounts of
the B vitamins.

➕ *Useful for boosting immunity and*
   *for cancer protection.*
➕ *Best eaten raw or very lightly*
   *cooked by stir-frying.*

## CAULIFLOWER
❶ ❷

*Energy per 100g / 3¹/₂oz 34 calories*
*Rich in vitamin C*

Cauliflower provides less beta-
carotene, riboflavin, and folic
acid than most brassicas, and these
essential constituents are easily
destroyed by cooking, so cut this
vegetable into small florets, wash well,
and eat as a *crudité*.

The white part of the cauliflower
is, in fact, the immature flowering
head. Eating some of the tender green
leaves closest to the flower increases
its beta-carotene and folic-acid
content. Cauliflower is also a good
source of vitamin C, which makes it
useful as a booster food for the
immune system.

➕ *Good for cancer protection and*
   *general immunity.*
➕ *Best eaten raw, slightly steamed, or*
   *boiled in minimal water.*

### FAST FOOD FACT

● People imagine that cauliflower
is a "windy" vegetable. In fact,
raw florets eaten with a dip of
live yogurt, olive oil, cider
vinegar, and crushed garlic makes
a great remedy for flatulence.

# SALAD VEGETABLES

*Prized for their vitamins A and C
and folate content*

CUCUMBER

The term salad is derived from the Latin word sal, meaning salt, since a salad originally meant merely something that was dipped in salt. The most widely used salad vegetable today is probably the lettuce, in its many forms, but salad vegetables range from the popular cucumber (low in calories, but with little nutritional value) to watercress (with its valuable nutritional, antibiotic, and cancer-protective properties) and asparagus: a treat to enjoy lightly cooked, when it is at its peak of freshness.

Green salad vegetables should not be placed in the category of "only for slimmers." Though they are indeed all very low in calories (mainly because of their high water content), they also contain a reasonable supply of nutrients and other medicinal properties. They are useful sources of vitamins A, C, and folate, some potassium and other minerals, including iodine. Generally the darker the color of the leaves, the more beta-carotene there is available, so don't throw away those rich, dark outer leaves. Some of these salad vegetables also act as diuretics, so they are helpful to relieve swelling or water retention. They combine successfully with an infinite variety of other vegetables and fruits to make interesting main or side dishes.

LETTUCE

CHICORY

# CHICORY ROOT, CHICORY, AND ENDIVE

② ③ ⑥ ⑧

CHICORY

*Energy per 3¹/₂oz / 100g 11 calories*
*Rich in vitamins A and C*

Wild chicory, also known as wild succory, has an ancient history as both a food and a medicine. The Egyptians, the Arabians, the Greeks, and the Romans all used it for both purposes. The most widely cultivated modern varieties are Witloof (broad-leaved, often blanched with yellow/green tips) and the curly endive, Ruffic.

Both chicory and cultivated endive are excellent sources of vitamins A (if not blanched) and C. They also contain some B vitamins and bitter terpenoids, which account for their stimulant effect on the liver and gall bladder. Both the leaves and roots have a gentle diuretic action as well as a mild therapeutic tonic effect. Chicory has an equally beneficial effect on the kidneys and is useful in urinary infections. Such an efficient eliminator of toxic wastes has obvious uses for those with skin problems and for sufferers from arthritis, rheumatism, and gout. Another study has shown chicory to have an anti-inflammatory action.

The coffee substitute made from ground chicory root has the benefit of not containing caffeine. Although there is little scientific proof of its value, it is known to be a mild diuretic, slightly sedative, and to stimulate the functioning of the glands in the digestive tract. Those who have difficulty digesting milk and milk products can benefit from drinking it, since the dried chicory-root powder helps to break down milk into much smaller particles.

✚ *Good for cleansing and detoxifying the digestive system.*

✚ *Useful as a mild diuretic, in jaundice, and as a liver stimulant.*

✚ *Best eaten raw or cooked.*

### FAST FOOD FACT

● Bruised chicory leaves make a good poultice for swollen joints and inflamed skin eruptions. Steam or microwave them until warm, then place on the affected spot for 15 minutes.

## ASPARAGUS

**2 6 8 9**

*Energy per standard portion 33 calories*
*Rich in vitamin C,*
*beta-carotene, and selenium*

You may imagine that asparagus is just a gourmet treat, but it has been cultivated for over 2,000 years and used medicinally since the sixteenth century Once you have eaten a portion of asparagus you will know that its major effect is that of a diuretic. Not only does it increase the amount of urine passed, but the smell of its active compound, asparagine, is noticeable in the urine within minutes of it being eaten. Because of this effect, asparagus has long been used by herbalists as a treatment for rheumatism and arthritis.

In the first century A.D. the Greek physician Dioscorides was using this plant for kidney and liver problems. Asparagus contains some fiber, which gives it a gentle laxative action, and it is also mildly sedative. It is also an excellent plant for women to eat around the time of their period, because it is helpful in reducing the discomfort of swollen breasts, fingers, and ankles.

Don't throw away the water in which you have cooked your asparagus—either drink it, or add it to soups or stocks for its diuretic value. And use woody parts of the asparagus stem to add flavor and medicinal value to soups.

➕ *Good for cystitis, fluid retention, and constipation.*
➕ *Helps arthritis and rheumatism.*
➕ *Best eaten steamed, with a little olive oil or melted butter.*
➖ *Not recommended for those with gout, because its purines may aggravate this condition.*

CELERIAC

## CELERIAC AND CELERY

④ ⑤ ⑥ ⑧ ⑨

CELERIAC
*Energy per 3¹/₂oz / 100g 18 calories*

CELERY
*Energy per standard portion 2 calories*
*Rich in folate*

Wild celery was highly valued by the Romans for its medicinal value, and cultivated varieties were developed by Italian gardeners in the Po Valley during the Middle Ages. It was introduced to Britain as a vegetable only toward the end of the seventeenth century, since when both wild and cultivated varieties have been popular with herbalists.

Celeriac is a turnip-rooted variety of celery, but it is the bulbous round stem that is eaten, rather than the stalks. Its smell is similar to that of celery but it has a less pronounced flavor. It may be eaten grated into fine matchsticks, either raw or parboiled, and served as salad with your favorite dressing. Nutritionally and chemically, celery and celeriac are similar, but the white bulb of celeriac and the blanched white celery stems do not contain beta-carotene, whereas dark-green celery stalks do. Celeriac is a rich source of folate, which makes it an excellent addition to salads for women planning pregnancy, and both

vegetables supply vitamin C, potassium, and fiber.

Hippocrates used celery in the treatment of nervous patients, and modern research in China and Germany has demonstrated that essential oils extracted from celery seed have a powerful calming effect on the central nervous system. These same oils have also been shown to reduce high blood pressure. ▶

### FAST FOOD FACTS

● One glass of mixed carrot and celery juice each day makes a good diuretic remedy.
● For gout and arthritis put half a teaspoon of celery seeds in a cup, fill with boiling water, cover and let stand for ten minutes. Pour the infusion through a fine tea strainer, add a little honey, as required, and drink one cup three times a day.

CELERY

**celeriac and celery continued**

The most traditional and still widely used benefit of celery is in the treatment of rheumatism, gout, and arthritis. A celery and celery-juice fast is used by the Japanese as a treatment for rheumatism, and celery cooked in milk and celery-seed tea are traditional Romany remedies for joint disorders. Its diuretic effect helps the body to get rid of excess fluid, together with uric acid, which aggravates the pain of all these joint disorders. The seeds are also an effective antiseptic and this, combined with their diuretic effect, makes them helpful in the treatment of cystitis and other urinary infections.

- ⊕ Good for rheumatism, arthritis, and gout.
- ⊕ Beneficial in reducing fluid retention and blood pressure.
- ⊕ Makes a good calming and antistress food.
- ⊕ Best eaten raw or juiced, but the strongest medicinal benefits come from the seeds.
- ⊖ Do not take celery-seed tea if you are pregnant or suffering from kidney disease. Use only culinary celery seed to make infusions— seeds for planting may be dressed with toxic chemicals.

# CUCUMBER
❸

*Energy per 3¹/₂oz / 100g 10 calories*
*Nutritionally poor*

It is quite extraordinary that this strange plant is so popular. Nutritionally, cucumber is devoid of virtually everything, save a tiny amount of vitamin A (10µg per 3¹/₂oz/100g) and a minute amount of iodine (3µg). It has a particularly high water content—96.4 percent—so is both refreshing and low in calories.

There is a long Indian, Middle Eastern, and eastern European tradition of pickling cucumbers to preserve them. Such pickles are delicious but of little nutritional value.

- ⊕ Therapeutic for the skin and eyes, and for dieters.
- ⊕ Best eaten with the skin on, well washed in warm water to remove the wax.

## FAST FOOD FACT

● Thin slices of cucumber placed over each eye are a soothing treat after a day of staring at a computer screen, driving, irritating sunshine, dust, or hay fever. Cucumber also makes an excellent astringent facial cleanser for oily skin.

## LETTUCE

*Energy per standard portion 7 calories*
*Rich in potassium and folic acid*

Lettuce is more than just 95 percent water. It contains vitamin C, beta-carotene, folic acid, some calcium, lots of potassium, a little iodine, and even a modest amount of iron. Any woman who is considering pregnancy should bear in mind that 3½oz/100g of lettuce provides more than a quarter of her daily need for folic acid.

There are many different varieties of lettuce and its nutritional value not only varies from type to type, but also depends on the time of the year and whether you eat the dark outer leaves or the very pale inner heart. As a general rule of thumb, the darker the leaf, the higher its beta-carotene content is likely to be.

All modern lettuces are descendants of the wild lettuce, much prized by the ancient Romans. The juice has the same properties as a very mild form of opium and, though cultivated lettuces are less potent, they still possess some of the sedative effects of their wild ancestor. A lettuce sandwich at bedtime is a far healthier alternative to sleeping pills. The combined sedative effects of the lettuce and the tryptophan released

by the digestion of carbohydrates ensure a good night's sleep.

Herbalists still use extracts from lettuce leaves to make sunburn lotion, while herbal medicines are made from the dried extracted "milk."

➕ *Good for insomnia, agitation, and bronchitis.*

➕ *Best eaten fresh and raw, as warm salad, or in soup.*

➖ *Where possible, choose organic lettuce or grow your own, since lettuce may accumulate synthetic nitrates from fertilizer.*

➖ *The milky sap that oozes from the stem of a lettuce can be very irritant to the eyes.*

### FAST FOOD FACT

● Whole large lettuce leaves boiled for a couple of minutes in water make an excellent poultice for boils, stings, and insect bites—apply them as hot as feels comfortable.

## WATERCRESS
**① ② ④ ⑦ ⑧**

*Energy per standard portion 4 calories*
*Rich in vitamins A, C, and E, and iodine*

Watercress is another member of the health-promoting Cruciferae family and should figure prominently in the diet of those at risk from cancer. It is a rich source of vitamins A, C, and E, the powerful antioxidants that protect against cardiovascular disease as well as some cancers.

For those who cannot give up smoking, chemo-prevention in the form of 1¾oz/50g of watercress, eaten at three meals each day for three days, in tests produced enough of the chemical phenethyl isothiocyanate to neutralize the important tobacco-specific lung-carcinogen NNK. This extraordinary protective chemical, also known as gluconasturtin, is released from watercress only when it is chewed or chopped.

But there is even more to this plant. Both watercress and nasturtium contain a benzyl mustard oil—similar compounds give "bite" to the related horseradish and radish—which research has shown to be powerfully antibiotic. But, unlike conventional antibiotics, those found in watercress and nasturtium are positively beneficial to the health of our gut. So eat plenty of watercress, add a nasturtium leaf or flower to your salad and you will greatly enhance your natural resistance. Respiratory and urinary infections in particular will benefit from a regular consumption of this salad vegetable.

➕ *Good for stomach infections, food poisoning, and anemia.*
➕ *Useful for cancer protection.*
➕ *Best eaten raw and well washed.*

### SUPER FOOD

● Add to all this the fact that watercress is also a useful source of iodine—essential for the proper functioning of the thyroid gland—and you will understand why it should not just be used as a garnish but should be eaten in generous quantities by all.

# EDIBLE SEAWEED

*Prized for its protein, soluble fiber, and mineral content*

**M**ost edible seaweeds are made up of the green, brown, and red varieties and, although often known as kelp, this term properly describes members of the Fucus species, most varieties of which occur only in northern seas and have traditionally been used in agriculture and medicine. Other varieties of seaweed, especially in China and Japan, have long been highly regarded as both food and medicine.

Although there are slight variations in the makeup of different varieties, the importance of adding seaweeds to the diet cannot be overstated. They are an excellent source of protein, but low in calories. They are full of soluble fiber, extremely rich in calcium and magnesium, a tremendous source of beta-carotene, rich in potassium, and exceptionally well supplied with iron and zinc. Seaweed is by far the richest source of natural iodine of all foods, a mineral that is essential for the normal functioning of the thyroid gland. For vegetarians and vegans, seaweeds are a real must, because of their vitamin $B_{12}$ content—$3\frac{1}{2}oz/100g$ providing many times the minimum daily requirement.

WAKAME

Folklore tells us that most seaweeds lower blood pressure, cure stomach ulcers, prevent goiter, and protect against some forms of cancer. In nutritional terms, these ancient remedies certainly work.

## KOMBU

*Energy per 3½oz / 100g 43 calories*
*Rich in vitamins A and C, and calcium*

This seaweed is often used to make nutritious soups and savoury dishes since it is a good source of calcium and vitamins A and C. It is a strongly flavored seaweed and one strip is normally enough to make 2½ cups/500ml of stock.

➕ *Good for anemia and boosting the immune system.*

➕ *Useful for the treatment and prevention of osteoporosis and weight loss.*

➕ *Best bought dried and soaked before use, unless it is being added to soups or stews.*

➖ *Contains a large amount of sodium, so is unsuitable for those with high blood pressure or on a low-salt diet.*

## NORI

*Energy per 3½oz / 100g 136 calories*
*Rich in protein and minerals*

Very rich in protein and minerals, nori is normally used as a garnish sprinkled onto savory dishes or cooked vegetables. It is often used in Japanese cooking to wrap up tasty morsels of savory ingredients.

➕ *Beneficial for lowering cholesterol, the treatment and prevention of osteoporosis and weight loss.*

➕ *Useful for anemia and for boosting the immune system.*

➕ *Best bought dried and soaked before use, unless it is being added to soups or stews.*

## WAKAME

❶ ❹ ❾

*Energy per 3¹/₂oz / 100g 71 calories*
*Rich in iron, calcium, and protein*

Wakame is similar to kombu and is high in protein, iron, and calcium. It is another good edible seaweed for beginners, because its taste is not dissimilar to that of green vegetables. It is used in Japanese cooking to make the nourishing and popular miso soup, which comprises mainly fermented soybean paste (see p.109).

➕ *Valuable for boosting the immune system and treating anemia.*
➕ *Good for lowering cholesterol, the treatment and prevention of osteoporosis, and weight loss.*
➕ *Best bought dried and soaked before use, unless it is being added to soups or stews.*

### OTHER SEAWEEDS

**ARAME** A good seaweed for beginners, it has a sweet flavor and is excellent in salads and soups.

**DULSE** This seaweed grows along the seaboard of North America, Iceland, and Ireland, and is definitely not a beginner's seaweed. No matter how long you cook it, it is always tough and has a strong, salty taste. The Irish make a traditional dulse soup which is, I believe, an acquired taste.

**HIZIKI** Sun-dried and shredded, with a sweet, delicate flavor, hiziki is immensely rich in calcium and iron—2oz/50g supplies enough for an adult's daily requirement of both these essential minerals.

**LAVER** One of the red seaweeds that grows off the coast of south Wales and Ireland, this can be gathered on the beach and for this reason has been a popular food in Wales for many hundreds of years. As a traditional Welsh breakfast it is rolled in oatmeal, fried, and served with eggs and bacon; however, be prepared for a very strong taste of the sea. The Welsh also use this seaweed to make laver bread—again, I am told, this is definitely an acquired taste and not recommended for seaweed novices.

If you gather any seaweed on the beach, do make sure beforehand that the shore is not polluted.

# FUNGI AND MEDITERRANEAN VEGETABLES

*Prized for their vitamin and antioxidant content*

This small group of vegetables, associated with the Mediterranean area though widely grown elsewhere, ranges from the richly nutritious and versatile tomato to the eggplant, which actually provides few nutrients. They offer exceptionally interesting flavors and textures, combined with very few calories (unless fried in oil).

While the eggplant does contain some potassium, small amounts of calcium, and vitamin A, its nutritional value is minimal unless eaten in very large quantities. On the other hand, tomatoes—one of the most widely consumed fruits (though generally classified with vegetables)—are rich in antioxidants like beta-carotene, as well as vitamins C and E, and are helpful in protecting against cardiovascular disease and some cancers. Though their wide commercial production is likely to continue to be detrimental to their flavor, they are highly versatile and can be used in many forms, from fresh to canned and juiced.

Olives are quite high in sodium, because of the processing that they undergo, but both they and their oil are prized for their antioxidant properties and monounsaturated fatty acids. As for mushrooms, recent research has claimed that they are surprisingly good sources of vitamin $B_{12}$, vitamin E, and high-quality protein.

TOMATO

SHIITAKE MUSHROOM

FIELD MUSHROOM

## MUSHROOMS

❶ ❹ ❺ ❼

*Energy per standard portion 5 calories*
*Rich in protein, vitamins B$_{12}$ and E*

Mushrooms, like truffles, are the edible portions of fungi—mushrooms appearing above ground, truffles below. Of course not all mushrooms are edible, some of them being highly poisonous and others simply unpalatable.

Our relationship with mushrooms is long and fascinating. The Egyptians believed they were a gift from the god Osiris, while the ancient Romans thought they resulted from the lightning thrown to earth by Jupiter during storms—which explained their sudden appearance, as if by magic. But there are written records going back to the Chinese Chow Dynasty, which reveal that mushrooms were already in use 3,000 years ago as both food and medicine. Researchers believe that this use can be traced back for at least another 3,000–4,000 years. In some parts of South America "magic mushrooms" have long been used as part of religious ceremonies because of their recognized hallucinogenic effects.

Whatever their history, we should all be eating more mushrooms than we do. They are a good source of easily absorbed, high-quality protein, containing more than most other vegetables, and are extremely low in calories, a scant 55 per 3½oz/100g, unless you choose to dip them in batter and deep-fry them. Mushrooms also contain some B vitamins, lots of phosphorus, and a large amount of potassium.

But it is their B$_{12}$ content that is extraordinary. Most textbooks state that mushrooms do not contain this vital vitamin, but the most up-to-date research reveals that mushrooms contain 0.32–0.65µg per gram of fresh mushroom. The same is true for vitamin E, which is listed as zero in mushrooms in most textbooks. Again, modern research reveals that most mushrooms are a rich source of this essential nutrient, 3½oz/100g providing more than the minimum daily requirement.

And the zinc content in mushrooms may be helpful in alleviating depression and anxiety. Zinc deficiency can be a major factor in depression, and antidepressants interfere with the body's uptake of zinc and exacerbate the problem. ▶

OYSTER MUSHROOM

BUTTON MUSHROOM

**mushrooms continued**

Dried mushrooms generally have a much fuller flavor than fresh ones and, although expensive, Italian, Japanese/Chinese. and French varieties are now widely available. Porcini, for example, are dried Cep mushrooms and have a very concentrated meaty flavor. Most dried varieties need to be soaked before being used, so rinse them well under running water, then cover with boiling water and leave to stand for at least half an hour. Don't throw away the water in which the mushrooms have been soaked—it makes a flavorsome stock for stews and soups.

For modern food researchers it is the Oriental mushrooms that are extremely interesting, with Shiitake, Reishi, and Maitake mushrooms commonly used medicinally in Japan and China. Shiitake are the source of traditional Chinese medicines for the treatment of depressed immune function. Reishi are believed to promote longevity and help treat liver diseases, high blood pressure, and asthma. Maitake mushrooms are also used for high blood pressure, cancer, liver disease, and the immune system.

➕ *Good for vegetarians and vegans, weight-loss programs, depression, and anxiety.*

➕ *Best eaten fresh (raw in salads, lightly sautéed, or added to soups, stews, and casseroles) or dried (well-washed, soaked, then used as fresh).*

➖ *If you go wild mushroom-gathering make sure that you have an excellent reference book and that you check with an expert before eating any edible fungi.*

## SUPER FOOD

● Two or three button mushrooms, or one reasonable-size field mushroom, will supply all the B$_{12}$ you need for an entire day, which is vital for vegetarians and even more so for vegans, since other plant sources of vitamin B$_{12}$ are very limited.

# TOMATOES

**1 3 4 9**

*Energy per standard portion 14 calories*
*Rich in vitamins C and E, and beta-carotene*

Tomatoes are probably one of the world's most important food crops and worldwide production is measured in tens of millions of tons each year. Unfortunately, ever-increasing commercial pressures, more sophisticated production methods, and genetic engineering do a disservice to this wonderful fruit. It is, by the way, botanically a fruit and not a vegetable.

The ancestral home of the tomato is the western coastal region of South America, stretching from Ecuador to Peru and Chile. Even in the high mountains, wild varieties abound— these are cherry tomatoes, the forerunners of all modern varieties. The first domestication probably occurred in Mexico, and tomatoes were subsequently introduced to Europe by the Spanish during the sixteenth century, after which they rapidly rampaged across southern Europe. As members of the Solanaceae family (which includes the deadly nightshade), tomatoes were at first treated with suspicion, but soon achieved their rightful place as a delicious and health-giving food.

Tomatoes are extremely rich in antioxidants, especially carotenoids like beta-carotene and lycopene, as well as vitamins C and E, making them good protectors of the cardiovascular system and against some forms of cancer. They are also extremely low in sodium and quite rich in potassium, so they are helpful in conditions like high blood pressure and fluid retention. A ripe tomato contains more than 200 volatile compounds that give it its unique aroma and flavor. Canned tomatoes lose very few of their nutrients but do gain some extra salt. If you are buying tomato juice or the traditional Italian passatta, be sure to choose low-salt varieties.

- **⊕** *Good for cancer protection, skin problems, and fertility.*
- **⊕** *Best eaten fresh and ripe, as purée, juice, or even canned.*
- **⊖** *Tomatoes may aggravate the pain and discomfort of rheumatoid arthritis.*
- **⊖** *Certain people find they have allergic reactions to tomatoes.*
- **⊖** *Green tomatoes may trigger migraines in some susceptible people.*

## EGGPLANTS

❶ ❹

*Energy per standard portion 20 calories*
*Contains some potassium, calcium, and vitamin A*

These beautiful, deep-purple fruit (which were probably originally egg-shaped, hence the name of eggplant) are part of the Solanaceae family of plants, which also includes potatoes, tomatoes, and deadly nightshade.

Originally from India and parts of Southeast Asia, eggplants have been grown for food and medicine for thousands of years. It is possible that their traditional use as a cancer treatment may have some real value after all, because they contain protease inhibitors, which are known to be anticancer chemicals.

This plant has been shown to reduce the amount of fat deposited in the arteries of animals fed on a high-fat diet, and eggplants should always be included in the normal dietary program for blood-pressure reduction. However, they are often eaten fried, which dramatically increases their calorie count.

Salting eggplants before cooking them helps to draw out their bitter juices and reduce their moisture. Slice them with a stainless-steel (not carbon-steel) knife, then sprinkle the slices with salt and put them to one

side for half an hour. Rinse under running water, then pat dry with paper towel and cook before the flesh discolors.

➕ *Help lower cholesterol levels and high blood pressure.*

➕ *May be cancer-protective.*

➕ *Best eaten when small, baked in the oven; larger fruit are best used for ratatouille.*

➖ *Best avoided by people with rheumatoid arthritis.*

### SUPER FOOD

● If you grow your own eggplants, the leaves can be warmed and used as a poultice to treat boils, burns, and abrasions. Take care, though, for the leaves are toxic and should only ever be used externally.

## OLVES

**1 3 4 5**

*Energy per standard portion 3 calories*
*Rich in antioxidants*

The olive tree is remarkable, since it can continue to bear fruit for a thousand years or more. It has been cultivated since prehistoric times in some Mediterranean areas and has always been intimately related to the nutritional, medicinal, religious, and cultural aspects of every civilization. Medicinally, olive leaves are extremely important. And as well as being grown for their fruit, olive trees are the source of the most nutritious of all vegetable oils—olive oil.

Olives straight from the tree are not edible, but are hard and extremely bitter. For this reason they have to be processed by pickling in heavily salted water. Consequently most table olives have a very high sodium content, up to 2,250mg per 3½oz/100g. The Greek method of treating olives differs in that it does not use an intermediate treatment with lye, a strong alkaline solution, but relies solely on brine. But whichever olives you choose, wash them thoroughly under running water for at least 15 minutes to remove as much salt as possible, then steep them in olive oil prior to eating.

Olives do provide a reasonable amount of vitamin E, a little fiber, and some monounsaturated oil, but little else of nutritional significance. It is the antioxidant compounds in the olive that give it, and its oil, such enormous health benefits. Oleaesterol is the most important of these protective substances.

➕ *Good for the skin, circulation, and the heart.*

➕ *Best eaten thoroughly rinsed to remove the high salt content.*

➖ *Avoid table olives if you have high blood pressure.*

### FAST FOOD FACT

● Olive leaves are known to contain oleuropein, which is powerfully antibacterial and antiviral. This same chemical is present throughout the olive tree and the fruit. Strong, bitter tea brewed from olive leaves can reduce blood pressure and increase natural immunity and has been used in the treatment of chronic fatigue syndrome.

# NUTS, SEEDS, AND LEGUMES

*Nuts and seeds*

*Legumes*

# NUTS, SEEDS, AND LEGUMES

The wide range of nuts, seeds, and legumes should be more widely used as part of a healthy balanced diet. Nuts in particular are a storehouse of energy and nutrients, suitable for both savory and sweet dishes, while legumes—except for the ubiquitous baked beans—are not widely recognized as providers of inexpensive and low-fat protein, which, with a little imagination, can be enjoyed in countless recipes.

PISTACHIO NUTS

Nuts and seeds were highly prized and grown by the Greeks, Romans, Chinese, South Americans, and Native North Americans for many centuries—and rightly so. They are rich sources of protein, fat, many minerals, and some fiber. Though the protein in nuts and seeds lacks some of the essential amino acids, these deficiencies can easily be made up from other sources. The total fat in nuts and some seeds exceeds that of fatty meat, but—with the exception of coconut and pine nuts—this is unsaturated fat, which can help to lower cholesterol. Nuts and seeds are all deficient in vitamin $B_{12}$ but do contain other B-complex vitamins. The many minerals in nuts can, however, be bound up with phytic

PUMPKIN SEEDS

LENTILS

*acid (or oxalic acid in peanuts), making it difficult for the body to absorb the minerals. Absorption can be improved by* roasting or cooking the nuts and seeds, or by eating a source of vitamin C at the same time. Nuts (particularly peanuts) and seeds can occasionally cause severe allergic reactions, which may prove fatal; great care should also be taken to ensure that young children do not choke on nuts.

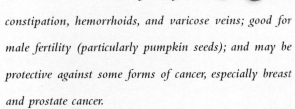

PEAS

*The fiber and polyunsaturated fats in nuts and seeds are helpful in treating diabetes and in protecting against coronary heart disease. Nuts and seeds are also beneficial for* constipation, hemorrhoids, and varicose veins; good for male fertility (particularly pumpkin seeds); and may be protective against some forms of cancer, especially breast and prostate cancer.

Legumes (also called pulses) are the dried seeds of leguminous plants, including beans, peas, and lentils. They are excellent sources of soluble fiber and protein, though they should be combined with wholegrain cereals, nuts, or seeds to make complete protein.

## ALMONDS
**❶ ❷ ❸ ❹**

*Energy per 3¹/₂oz / 100g 612 calories*
*Rich in protein and minerals*

The almonds most commonly eaten are the sweet ones. Almonds are rich in fat and vital minerals such as zinc, magnesium, potassium, and iron, as well as some B vitamins. Since they are also high in oxalic and phytic acids, which combine with these minerals to carry them out of your body, you should eat them at the same time as vitamin C-rich foods for maximum absorption. Of all nuts, almonds contain the most calcium, and 20 per-cent protein—weight for weight, one-third more protein than eggs. Almond oil is especially soothing to the skin.

⊖ *Bitter almonds contain toxic prussic acid and should never be eaten raw.*

### FAST FOOD FACT

● Almond milk is sustaining and soothing for invalids. Soak 1³/₄oz/50g of whole almonds in tepid water, then skin them. Pound with part of 5 cups/1l of water. Add to the rest of the water, stir in one tablespoon of honey, strain and drink.

## MACADAMIAS
**❶ ❷ ❹**

*Energy per 3¹/₂oz / 100g 748 calories*
*Rich in fiber, protein, iron, and zinc*

Although originally an Australian plant, this is now a major cultivated crop in Hawaii. It is rare to find macadamias as fresh nuts, since they are nearly always roasted and salted. They are very high in fat, so they go rancid quickly. They are a reasonable source of fiber, protein, iron, and zinc, but very high in salt.

## SUNFLOWER SEEDS
**❶ ❷ ❹**

*Energy per 3¹/₂oz / 100g 581 calories*
*Rich in protein and vitamin E*

Sunflower seeds are extremely nutritious, as well as tasting good. They provide large amounts of protein, B vitamins, iron, zinc, potassium, and selenium and are one of the best sources of vitamin E. Sprinkle them on savory dishes or add them to salads.

## PECANS
**① ② ④**

*Energy per 3¹/₂oz / 100g 689 calories*
*Rich in protein and unsaturated fats*

Pecans are a good source of protein, very high in unsaturated fats, and contain a reasonable quantity of fiber. They also provide modest amounts of calcium, magnesium, iron, and zinc, and 3¹/₂oz/100g will provide more than the recommended daily allowance of vitamin E.

## BRAZIL NUTS
**① ② ④**

*Energy per 3¹/₂oz / 100g 682 calories*
*Rich in selenium*

Brazil nuts are high in fat and go rancid very quickly. Buy only the amount you need, from a reputable supplier. They are one of the richest sources of the essential mineral selenium—a few nuts each day should give you all you need to protect against heart disease and cancer.

## CHESTNUTS
**① ② ④**

*Energy per 3¹/₂oz / 100g 170 calories*
*Rich in fiber*

You can buy these wonderful nuts with or without their shells, fresh or dried, ground into meal, and even canned, vacuum-packed, or frozen. They must not be confused with the poisonous horse chestnut, which is used in herbal medicine.

Chestnuts must be cooked before eating—in Britain traditionally being roasted over an open fire—but can also be used in sweet and savory dishes, cooked with vegetables, in soups or traditional turkey stuffing. Dried and ground into flour they are excellent for people suffering from celiac disease or indeed any form of gluten intolerance, since they are gluten-free.

Chestnuts are much lower in calories than other nuts because they contain far less fat, but they are also low in protein. They do supply some vitamin E, potassium, and vitamin B₆.

### SUPER FOOD

● Most nuts (except coconut and pine nuts) contain linoleic acid, which counteracts cholesterol deposits and is thought to protect against heart disease.

## SESAME SEEDS

❶ ❷ ❹ ❺

*Energy per 3¹/₂oz / 100g 598 calories*
*Rich in calcium and B vitamins*

These have been popular for centuries in the Middle East and the Far East, where they have a reputation as an aphrodisiac, which may be because of their vitamin E and iron content. They are an exceptional source of calcium and a very good source of protein and magnesium. They are also rich in B vitamins, especially niacin and folate.

In the Middle East sesame seeds are traditionally used to make a popular spread called tahini, a thick paste, which is similar in texture to peanut butter, but without the lumps. Sprinkled on top of, or added to, cakes and especially wholewheat bread, they add lots of nutrients and a distinctive nutty flavor. They are an essential ingredient in Asian cooking, and sesame-seed oil is excellent both for salads and wok cooking.

## COCONUTS

❶ ❷ ❹

*Energy per 3¹/₂oz / 100g 351 calories*
*Rich in fiber*

Coconuts are delicious eaten fresh and the "milk" is refreshing, although not very nutritious. When desiccated (dried), coconut can be used in cooking, but is often compressed into hard slabs of coconut cream. However, any coconut is much higher in saturated fats than other nuts. It is a good source of fiber and other nutrients, but should be eaten in moderation.

## HAZELNUTS

❶ ❷ ❹

*Energy per 3¹/₂oz / 100g 650 calories*
*Rich in vitamin E*

An excellent source of protein, fiber and magnesium, hazelnuts also contain iron, zinc, and lots of vitamin E—3¹/₂oz / 100g provide nearly a week's worth. They are very low in salt, good eaten on their own, used in cooking, or as hazelnut butter.

## PINE NUTS

**❶ ❷ ❹**

*Energy per 3¹/₂oz / 100g 688 calories*
*Rich in vitamin E, potassium,*
*and protein*

These are a great Mediterranean delicacy and a key ingredient of traditional Italian pesto sauce. They are an excellent source of protein although quite high in fats. They supply a little fiber but important amounts of magnesium, iron, and zinc and lots of vitamin E and potassium.

## PISTACHIO

**❶ ❷ ❹**

*Energy per 3¹/₂oz / 100g 601 calories*
*Rich in vitamin E and potassium*

It is almost impossible to buy these delicious nuts unsalted, and salted pistachios contain far too much sodium. Pistachios are a good protein source, contain valuable amounts of fiber, with some iron, zinc, and vitamin A, as well as significant amounts of vitamin E and potassium.

## PUMPKIN SEEDS

**❶ ❷ ❹ ❺**

*Energy per 3¹/₂oz / 100g 569 calories*
*Rich in iron, phosphorus, and zinc*

In spite of their 569 calories per 3¹/₂oz/100g, these seeds are very nutritious, almost a quarter of their weight being protein. They are also lower in fats than most other nuts or seeds, a good source of fiber, magnesium, and potassium, an excellent source of iron, phosphorus, and zinc, and contain a little vitamin A. The seeds can also be used to make an extremely safe treatment for tapeworm (see p.65), one of many traditional and herbal remedies for parasites that actually works.

### SUPER FOOD

● Because of their high zinc content, pumpkin seeds are particularly valuable for men. Zinc is essential for the production of fertile sperm, as well as being a specifically protective substance for the prostate gland, so a handful of pumpkin seeds a day is good health insurance.

## PEANUTS
**❶ ❷ ❹**

*Energy per 3¹/₂oz / 100g 564 calories*
*Rich in protein, vitamin D, and iodine*

Peanuts are extremely nutritious whether eaten raw or roasted, but not as healthy when salted. They are high in protein, 3¹/₂oz/100g providing nearly half a day's requirements, and comparatively low in fat. They are a good source of fiber, magnesium, iron, and zinc, and an excellent source of vitamin D and a valuable source of iodine.

## WALNUTS
**❶ ❷ ❹**

*Energy per 3¹/₂oz / 100g 688 calories*
*Rich in folate*

Wet walnuts are a great delicacy. But whether eaten fresh, chopped into cakes, pickled, or pressed into oil, walnuts are a healthy food. Low in sodium and saturated fat, high in polyunsaturated and monounsaturated fats, they provide protein, a small quantity of zinc, vitamin E, and useful amounts of folate.

## CASHEW NUTS
**❶ ❷ ❹**

*Energy per 3¹/₂oz / 100g 573 calories*
*Rich in potassium, folate,*
*and nicotinic acid*

Plain roasted cashews are delicious and rich in heart-protecting monounsaturated fat. They are also a good source of potassium, nicotinic acid, and folate. Cashew-nut butter, though high in calories, is a very good source of nutrients. Cashew trees grow in Brazil, and the nuts hang underneath the fruit—the rain-forest-dwelling Brazilians preferring the fruit to the nuts. Cashews are always sold shelled and roasted, because the roasting destroys the highly caustic oil between the two layers of its shell.

➖ *Salted cashew nuts are a real danger food in terms of high blood pressure and heart disease, 3¹/₂oz/100g providing more than half the recommended daily intake of salt.*

# LEGUMES

*Prized for their protein and soluble fiber content*

Legumes—*including the whole range of dried and green beans, as well as sprouting beans and soy products—are a marvelous source of soluble fiber and can be combined with*

*wholegrains to make an indispensable alternative to meat. They also make great contributions to energy supply; for example, in some areas of sub-Saharan Africa they comprise 11–17 percent of total energy, and in China 10 percent.*

*STRING BEANS*

*Dry legumes are the richest plant source of protein and contain 6–11 percent protein by cooked weight—in this regard they are comparable to meat. They are also good sources of vitamins, minerals, and bioactive compounds such as isoflavones, which may be protective against breast cancer. The immature, or green, beans lack the concentrated sources of protein, starch, and some minerals, but they are higher in vitamins A and C. Sprouted beans such as mung, chickpea, alfalfa, and aduki are all excellent sources of vitamin C.*

*Legumes are consumed worldwide in a wide variety of ways; examples include Japanese and Chinese beancurd (tofu), Chinese mung-bean sprouts, Mexican chili and refried beans, Indian dahl, Middle Eastern falafel and humus, Cuban black beans and rice, Boston baked beans, Italian minestrone, and Swedish pea soup. You simply cannot afford to miss trying—and enjoying— this nutritious food group.*

BLACK-EYED BEANS

STRING BEANS

## GREEN BEANS

② ③ ④ ⑧ ⑨

FAVA BEANS
*Energy per 3¹/₂oz / 100g 58 calories*

STRING BEANS
*Energy per 3¹/₂oz / 100g 24 calories*

POLE BEANS
*Energy per 3¹/₂oz / 100g 22 calories*
*Rich in potassium and folate*

String and pole beans both contain vitamins A and C, making them useful for skin disorders; they also contain sufficient fiber to help with constipation. Fava beans, which alone can be eaten raw, are a good source of protein and, puréed with olive oil and garlic, nutritious food for convalescents. They are also a good source of pantothenic acid, and are advocated as an aid to male potency.

Beans are rich in potassium, very low in sodium, and have a mild diuretic effect. They are also rich in folate, so they make good food for women who are planning pregnancy.

➕ *Good for digestive problems, skin disorders and male sexual potency.*
➕ *Pole and string beans best eaten lightly steamed; fava beans raw, steamed, or puréed.*
➖ *Fava bean pods are on the "forbidden food" list for those taking MAOIs, antidepressant drugs.*

## SOYBEANS

① ④

*Energy per 3¹/₂oz / 100g 141 calories*
*Rich in protein and antioxidants*

Soybeans contain the most complete protein and lend themselves to the production of a range of nutritious products (see p.109). But it is the anticancer activity of the soybean that makes it so valuable. Its antioxidant content protects against free-radical damage, which can lead to heart and circulatory disease as well as to cancer. Japanese studies have shown a risk reduction of around one-third for stomach cancer simply by eating a daily portion of miso soup. Soybeans also offer protection against the hormone-linked cancers—breast, ovarian, and cervical—because of their phytoestrogen chemicals, known as isoflavones. The most recent of these to be isolated is genistein, known to limit the growth of cancer cells.

➕ *Useful cancer-protective food.*
➕ *Good for the heart and for circulatory disease.*
➕ *Best eaten as tofu, soy milk, soy cheese, soy sauce, or miso.*
➖ *Soybeans are a common food allergen and may cause indigestion or headaches in some people.*

TOFU

MISO

# BEAN CURD

**1 2 4**

TOFU

*Energy per 3¹/₂oz / 100g 261 calories*
*Rich in protein*

Soy foods have been eaten for centuries in Asia and are being increasingly accepted as a meat substitute for the ever-growing number of vegetarians in the Western world. In this form they are usually presented as soy sausages, soy chicken nuggets, soy cubes that resemble beef, and soy hamburger substitute. There is ample evidence that the combined effects of eating less meat and more soybean reduces the risk of getting stomach cancer, raised cholesterol, and heart disease.

Miso (fermented soybean paste) is produced from cooked soybeans mixed with rice, barley, or more soybeans that have been fermented. The mixture is left to ferment further, producing a thick, nutritious paste.

Soy milk for drinking is made by soaking, pulverizing, cooking, then filtering the beans. It is further refined and then has sweeteners, oil, flavorings, and salt added. Extra calcium is often added, and it may then be turned into soy cheese. Both are excellent substitutes for anyone allergic to dairy products.

Tofu (soybean curd) is made from soy milk, which is coagulated, then the whey is discarded and the curds pressed to form the tofu. It is highly absorbent and takes on the flavor of other ingredients with which it is being cooked.

The Japanese do not eat tofu in huge quantities, but use small amounts with rice as their staple energy source, together with a wide range of vegetables, including seaweed. This is important, because it is believed that soy may contain substances that reduce the function of the thyroid gland, while seaweed is rich in iodine, which stimulates the thyroid.

Overall the benefits of soy and its products are enormous.

- ✚ *Good for cancer and cancer protection.*
- ✚ *An excellent substitute for those with a milk allergy.*
- ✚ *Good for vegetarians and diabetics.*
- ✚ *Beneficial for heart disease, high blood pressure, and high cholesterol.*
- ✚ *Useful for both constipation and for gallstones.*

## DRIED BEANS

**❶ ❹ ❽**

ADUKI BEANS
*Energy per 3¹/₂oz/100g 123 calories*

CHICKPEAS
*Energy per 3¹/₂oz/100g 42 calories*

BLACK-EYED BEANS
*Energy per 3¹/₂oz/100g 116 calories*

NAVY BEANS
*Energy per standard portion 57 calories*

LIMA BEANS
*Energy per standard portion 62 calories*

KIDNEY BEANS
*Energy per 3¹/₂oz/100g 123 calories*

PINTO BEANS
*Energy per standard portion 82 calories*
*Rich in soluble fiber and minerals*

Dried beans have been a staple survival food since time immemorial. Excluding fruit and vegetables, there are only about 50 species of plants that make a major contribution to people's diet worldwide. Most of them are cereals, but second come the legumes—the family that contains all the beans, or pulses, as they are also known.

Except for the obviously oily members of the bean family, like the groundnut and the peanut, beans are low in fat and salt, contain no cholesterol, but are a rich source of proteins, starches, vitamins, minerals, and fiber. They have two other great advantages—they are extremely cheap and can be stored for far longer than nearly any other food. They are some of the most nutritious, satisfying, versatile, healthy, and, with a little imagination, delicious foods that money can buy.

Beans are a great source of the best sort of fiber, the soluble kind—two tablespoons of cooked kidney beans give you four times as much as one slice of wholewheat bread. This fiber combines with cholesterol and helps to eliminate it from the body. At the same time, beans contain nearly as much protein, pound for pound, as steak, but at a fraction of the cost. None of the beans contains all the essential amino acids that make up protein, but this doesn't matter if they are eaten as part of a mixed diet. Strict vegetarians have to remember to combine beans with one or more of the other main food groups—dairy products, nuts and seeds, or cereals—at the same meal. It is particularly important that vegetarians do eat beans as a source of protein, because they contain such substantial amounts of folic acid, lack of which may cause birth defects and anemia. ▶

CHICKPEAS

LIMA BEANS

**dried beans continued**

Beans are an excellent source of the minerals calcium, iron, copper, zinc, phosphorus, potassium, and magnesium. Because of their high potassium and low sodium content, they represent an ideal food for anyone with high blood pressure or for people needing a low-sodium diet.

For diabetics, beans comprise an excellent form of starch, since they are easily but slowly digestible and convert to relatively small amounts of sugar. They are also generally cancer-protective, since they contain protease inhibitors, which help prevent the development of cancerous cells.

Lentils, mung beans, black-eyed beans, and split peas do not need to be soaked, but all other beans should be soaked for at least six to eight hours before cooking. Kidney beans must be boiled hard for ten minutes, strained, then simmered until tender to destroy a toxin called lectin, which can cause stomach upsets. If you cook beans with salt, the skins become tougher, less digestible, and more available to gut bacteria, which cause fermentation. Not putting a lid on the saucepan keeps the skins soft and digestible. Canned beans should be well rinsed under running water to remove excess salt.

The German name for the herb summer savory is the "bean herb" and adding some of this herb when cooking beans reduces flatulence (adding fennel or caraway seeds will have the same effect).

- ✚ *Good for the heart, circulation, and high blood pressure.*
- ✚ *Beneficial as cancer-protective foods.*
- ✚ *Good for healthy bowel function.*
- ✚ *Best eaten cooked or canned, but watch out for added salt.*

### BEAN FACTS

**Aduki beans** are good for fiber, magnesium, potassium, and zinc.
**Baked beans**, or navy beans, are a rich source of fiber and a reasonable source of iron, selenium, and iodine (but watch out for added salt).
**Black-eyed beans** (peas) are good for fiber and selenium and excellent for folate.
**Chickpeas** are good for fiber, calcium, iron, and zinc.
**Kidney beans** are excellent for fiber, potassium, and zinc.
**Lima beans** are useful for fiber, potassium, and iron.
**Mung beans** are slightly lower in starch, but good for folate.
**Navy beans** contain fiber and iron.

## BEAN SPROUTS

**❶ ❺**

*Energy per standard portion 5 calories*
*Rich in vitamin C*

Bean sprouts—not just traditional mung beans, but many other types of sprouted beans too—are a wonderful source of vitamins and minerals. They have been described as "the most live, pure, nutritious, food imaginable." They are also cheap and easy to grow. When you sprout beans, what you produce is an enormously enhanced package of the nutrients already there. In one study, only small amounts of vitamin C were found in wheat grains, but this increased by 600 percent over the next few days. And 3½oz/100g of bean sprouts provides all the vitamin C necessary for two days.

You can plant bean sprouts any day of the year (but buy only organic beans and seeds) and harvest them fresh for instant consumption: aduki, mung, and soybeans, alfalfa, sesame,

and fenugreek seeds, barley and wheat grains, and chickpeas are all easy to sprout. Sort the seeds, removing any obviously damaged ones. Soak them in ample tepid water for 12 hours, then drain. Put them in a jam jar and cover with cheesecloth kept in place with an elastic band. Store in a warm, dark place. Rinse the seeds with fresh water at least a couple of times a day, then dry them well. You will be ready to harvest this powerhouse of nutrition within two to six days.

➕ *Excellent for cancer and cancer protection.*

➕ *Good for anyone with a compromised immune system.*

➕ *Beneficial for all chronic fatigue states.*

➕ *Best eaten fresh and raw; combine well with other vegetables for stir-frying.*

➖ *Bean sprouts may produce an allergic reaction in those with systemic Lupus erythematosus.*

### SUPER FOOD

● Bean sprouts are an ideal food for cancer patients, for those who are anxious to boost their immune defenses, and for conditions needing first-class nutrition.

## PEAS

❷ ❺

*Energy per 100g / 3½oz  83 calories*
*Rich in thiamin and folic acid*

Nothing matches the wonderful flavor of homegrown peas straight from the garden. In fact, in England, peas are the most popular vegetable of all. Unfortunately, from a nutritional point of view, canned peas take the lion's share of the market.

Green peas provide an excellent source of thiamin (vitamin $B_1$), with 5oz/150g supplying more than a day's need. They are also a valuable source of folic acid, supply useful amounts of vitamins A and C and protein, although they need to be combined with cereals such as rice, pasta, or bread to make complete protein.

Because the sugars in peas start to convert into starches as soon as the pods are picked from the vine, many people prefer the sweeter taste of frozen peas, and modern technology allows peas to be frozen almost instantly after harvesting, conserving both their sweetness and their vitamin C content; they can be kept frozen for up to a year without nutritional losses.

The now-popular snow peas are similar in composition to green peas, but by eating the entire pod, the amounts of vitamins A and C that you consume increase considerably.

All forms of peas (together with chickpeas, which are also a legume and are used in a similar way to peas by different peoples) are excellent sources of dietary fiber.

➕ *Good for stress, tension, and the digestion.*
➕ *Best eaten very fresh or frozen.*
➖ *Peas contain quite large amounts of phytate, which can reduce the bio-availability of minerals such as iron, calcium, and zinc, so don't make peas the only green vegetable you ever eat.*

### FAST FOOD FACT

🔴 **A large bag of frozen peas makes the cheapest reusable ice pack for the treatment of strains, sprains, bruises, frozen shoulder, tennis elbow, etc. Always put a thin layer of cloth between your skin and the frozen peas. Mark the peas in indelible ink so that they don't get eaten by mistake.**

GREEN AND RED LENTILS

RED LENTILS

## LENTILS

④ ⑤

*Energy per standard portion 41 calories*
*Rich in protein, starch, and B vitamins*

Lentils have been used as food by people since prehistory—evidence of them having been found in excavated prehistoric sites in Switzerland. Like all legumes, lentils supply abundant amounts of protein and starch and are a good source of the B vitamins. They also contain significant amounts of iron, zinc, and calcium. The downside is their phytic acid content, which makes it more difficult to absorb these minerals. Eating a good source of vitamin C together with lentils increases the amount of iron absorbed.

Although lentils are rich in protein, this protein does not contain all of the essential amino acids. But combining lentils with cereals such as rice or wholewheat bread provides the body with complete protein—and vegetarian Indians always eat rice or bread as an accompaniment to their meal.

The most usual forms of lentils are red, yellow, green, or brown and there is little nutritional difference between them. Unique among legumes, lentils do not need to be soaked before cooking. Their high fiber content makes lentils an excellent protector against bowel cancer, and their abundant supply of B vitamins, especially niacin, makes them the perfect food for anyone who is suffering from excessive stress or severe mental exhaustion.

➕ *Useful for vegetarians and diabetics.*
➕ *Good for reducing cholesterol, stress, and nervous exhaustion.*
➕ *Best eaten either cooked on their own or used to make traditional Indian dahl.*
➖ *The purines in lentils can cause uric acid salts to be deposited in the joints, so lentils are best avoided by those with gout.*

# MEAT, FISH, AND SHELLFISH

*Meat and organ meat*

*Poultry*

*Game and game birds*

*Fish and shellfish*

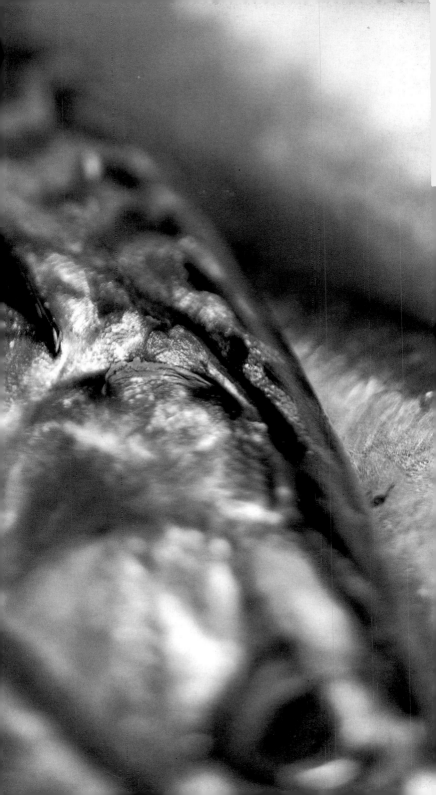

# MEAT, FISH, AND SHELLFISH

Despite the poor press received by the meat industry in recent years, meat remains a very valuable source of protein and plays a major role in the prevention of anemia, because of its iron and zinc. So all official recommendations in recent years still include meat as part of a nutritious, healthy diet, but recommend that you try to substitute fatty meat with lean meat, poultry without skin, and all kinds of nutritious fish and shellfish.

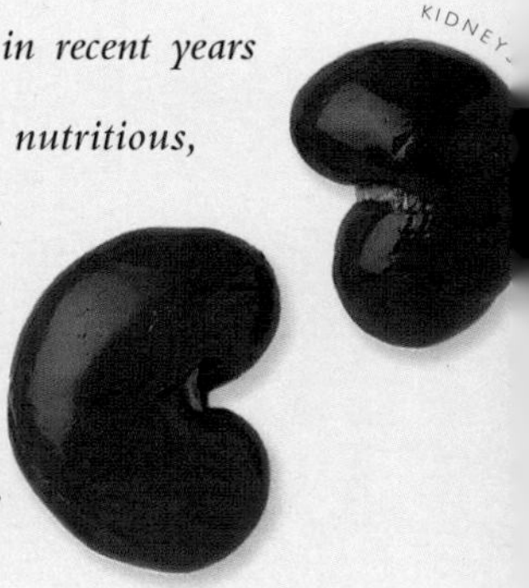

KIDNEY

Meat and meat products are known to be major sources in industrialized countries of saturated fat—a high intake of which is strongly associated with cancer, cardiovascular disease, and obesity. But despite these scares and recent well-publicized E. coli and BSE outbreaks, red meat (from beef, lamb, and pork) continues to be central to most diets in developed societies. As a general rule, meat consumption increases with economic development; for example, between 1980 and 1987 meat intake in Japan rose dramatically from around $^2/_3$ oz/18g per person per day to $2^1/_2$ oz/71g.

BEEF

Meat is an excellent source of protein, a rich source of vitamins $B_6$ and $B_{12}$, and of easily absorbable iron, zinc, selenium, and fatty acids. Organ meats (kidney and liver) comprise an extremely rich source of iron and vitamin A; small amounts of organ meat should be more widely used in our diets, although pregnant women should avoid liver, because of its high vitamin A content.

Fish too has suffered from concerns about pollution of the oceans and rivers in which it is found, and about the contamination with heavy metals of some fish—for example, tuna—in some parts of the world. Consumption of fish and shellfish varies widely worldwide, depending on local tradition, the availability of good fresh fish, and public confidence in its handling and preparation.

VENISON

Weight for weight, fish is an excellent source of protein, since there is little waste. It contains relatively lower levels of B vitamins, iron, and zinc than meat and poultry, but oily fish are a rich source of retinol (vitamin A), vitamin D, omega-3 fatty acids (thought to be protective against coronary heart disease), and calcium (if the fish bones are eaten). Shellfish are valued for their high selenium and iron content.

## BEEF

❺

CORNED BEEF
*Energy per 3¹/₂oz /100g 217 calories*

STEWED GROUND BEEF
*Energy per 3¹/₂oz /100g 229 calories*

BROILED, LEAN RUMP STEAK
*Energy per 3¹/₂oz /100g 168 calories*
*Rich in protein and minerals, vitamin $B_{12}$, and other B vitamins*

Beef has traditionally been one of the most highly sought-after of all meats. Defined by the *Oxford English Dictionary* as the flesh of ox, bull, or cow, it gets its name from the Latin *bos, bovis*. In early English history, beef was reserved for the ruling Normans.

Throughout the world about 237 million head of beef and calves and 11 million head of buffalo are produced annually, and beef is, without doubt, the universal meat. There is no denying its nutritional benefit: it supplies most nutritional needs except fiber, although some constituents such as calcium, vitamin C, and folate are present only in small amounts. Beef is a good source of trace elements such as iodine, manganese, zinc, cobalt, selenium, nickel, chromium, molybdenum, fluorine, vanadium, and silicon. The presence of these is dependent on the soil on which the animals graze, or on the components of manufactured feed.

The growing trend toward vegetarianism in recent years and concerns about the nutritional effects of eating beef, have led to white meats replacing beef, to a certain extent, as the major source of animal protein in both the United States and Britain. All but the very leanest cuts of beef can contain up to 20 percent by weight of saturated fat and there is certainly a growing awareness of the connection between high levels of meat consumption and raised blood cholesterol levels. Furthermore, the link between cancer of the large bowel (colon) and prostate and copious amounts of red meat in the diet is good reason to make the consumption of beef an occasional treat, rather than a daily occurrence. Both the World Health Organization (WHO) and the Harvard School of Public Health suggest that beef should be eaten only a few times a month. ▶

**beef continued**

The nutritional composition of different sorts of beef varies widely. For example, 3½oz/100g of corned beef contains 950mg of sodium, compared with 320mg in stewed ground beef and only 56mg in broiled, lean rump steak. The total fat in corned beef is 12.1g, in ground beef 15.2g, but in steak only a meager 6g.

The way beef is cooked is an important factor in nutritional terms. Trimming excessive visible fat before cooking reduces the total fat in the finished dish. Joints should be roasted on a trivet, so that the fat drips into the pan below. Steaks and chops should be cooked in the same way. Overcooking meat on the barbecue leads to the greatest production of carcinogens, the highest levels of all being found in combination with the highest fat content. Take especial care with lower-cost sausages and burgers, which contain more fat.

There have been a number of scares about beef in recent years, the most alarming in Britain being BSE or "mad cow disease," which has been linked to the new strain of Creutzfeldt-Jakob disease (CJD) in humans. Rather more insidious is the risk of contamination of beef by the illegal use of chemicals, and although antibiotics have long been banned as an animal-feed additive, there are signs that illegal hormones are being used on a wide scale all over Europe, while in the United States some laboratory-produced "natural" hormones are allowed as growth promoters.

➕ *Contains a broad variety of essential nutrients, especially iron and zinc.*

➕ *Good for anemia, stress, and other nervous disorders.*

➕ *Best eaten broiled, roasted on a trivet, or stewed.*

➖ *The undercooked burger can harbor harmful bacteria, including E. coli, 0157:H7, VTEC.*

### E. COLI

● *E. coli* 0157:H7, VTEC is believed to affect more than 20,000 Americans each year. Over 500 people became ill in 1993 and several of the affected children died. And a major outbreak in Scotland in 1996, followed by a second in early 1997, left at least 20 people dead and many seriously ill. The risk of contracting *E. coli* can be reduced by thoroughly cooking burgers.

## GELATINE

*Energy per standard portion 10 calories*
*Of limited nutritional value*

Gelatine is the result of prolonged boiling of animal skin, tendons, and ligaments. These contain collagen, which is mostly protein, but it is a form of protein that is very difficult for the human system to digest.

It is gelatine that makes a stew thick and "hearty," and in the presence of other forms of protein, such as beans, split peas, barley, or lentils, gelatine can provide reasonable protein. The main commercial use for it is as a setting agent in many pre-prepared products such as trifles, mousses, and similar desserts (vegetarians beware!) and as the main ingredient of jellies and aspic. Because it is so cheap to produce, more gelatine is used by the food industry than any other form of setting agent.

Gelatine is the subject of two old wives' tales: eating cubes of raw Jello does not give you worms, nor does it strengthen your fingernails.

⊕ *Useful as a setting agent and for thickening stews.*
⊖ *All meat jellies are very easily contaminated by bacteria, so they need to be handled and kept with great care.*

## VEAL
❺

*Energy per 3¹/₂oz / 100g 109 calories*
*Rich in protein and B vitamins*

Veal has become a highly controversial meat in recent years, mainly because of the way calves are reared and transported. For those without any qualms about eating three-month-old baby cattle, veal provides a good source of nutrients. It contains less than half the fat and fewer calories than lean beef, though it is an excellent source of protein, zinc, potassium, and B vitamins.

Milk-fed veal supplies only half the iron present in ordinary beef, though calves that have been naturally reared on their mothers' milk and allowed to graze normally produce much darker meat, which is only slightly less rich in iron than mature beef.

Hugely popular throughout northern Europe, veal is commonly served coated with egg and breadcrumbs, then fried, which increases its fat content dramatically.

⊕ *Good for high-protein, low-fat diets.*
⊕ *Best eaten roasted or pan-fried, in minimal quantities of vegetable oil.*

## LAMB
⑤

*Energy per 3¹/₂oz / 100g 156 calories*
*Rich in protein and B vitamins*

Like all meat, lamb is an excellent source of protein, easily absorbed iron, and zinc and B vitamins. Of all the farmed animals, lamb is least likely to be contaminated with antibiotic residues or to have been fed on reconstituted animal protein. New-season spring lamb is always the most tender and has the lowest fat content, but modern breeds are all generally lower in fat.

To dry-roast lamb, seal the meat all over in hot oil and remove from the pan. Sauté lightly garlic, bay leaves, peppercorns, and rosemary together in a pan. Add a little red wine and return the lamb to the pan. Cover and cook slowly, checking the fluid level regularly. When almost done, remove the lid and turn up the heat. Serve with green lentils.

The amount of fat that you get with your lamb depends on the cut, how it is cooked, and what you actually eat of it. Ideally, most of the fat should be removed before cooking and any that is left on the meat should be avoided.

➕ *Good for anemia, those on high-protein diets, and for loss of appetite.*
➕ *Best eaten broiled, roasted on a rack or, best of all, dry-roasted in the Greek/Middle Eastern style.*

### FAT CONTENT

**BROILED CHOPS**
Eaten without fat: 12.3g fat/100g
Eaten with fat:      29g fat/100g

**ROAST LEG**
Eaten without fat: 8.1g fat/100g
Eaten with fat:     18g fat/100g

**ROAST SHOULDER**
Eaten without fat: 11.2g fat/100g
Eaten with fat:     26g fat/100g

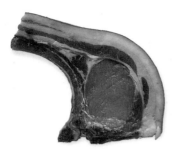

## PORK

Energy per 3½oz / 100g 122 calories
Rich in B vitamins and iron

There is a popular misconception that pork is a "fatty" meat, whereas in fact modern breeds produce meat that contains less fat than beef or lamb, and very little more than chicken, if eaten without skin. Naturally the type of cut and the way it is cooked can make an enormous difference. Delicious though crackling is, it is nothing more than crispy fat and it is far healthier to remove as much fat as possible before cooking any cut of pork.

There is no doubt that pork is an extremely good source of nutrients, containing large amounts of thiamin ($B_1$), niacin, riboflavin ($B_2$), and zinc. It is also a reasonably good source of vitamin $B_6$, phosphorus, and haem iron, which is more easily absorbed and used by the body than ordinary iron. The abundance of B vitamins makes pork a good food for all stress and nervous problems, while the $B_6$ and zinc certainly help with PMS, and the zinc is particularly useful for the maintenance of healthy sperm. The beneficial levels of iron are useful in the prevention and treatment of anemia, and in addition to all this pork is an excellent source of complete protein—a 3½oz/100g serving of lean pork providing more than half the daily requirement.

Some of the byproducts of pork are interesting medically, especially the hormones such as pig insulin and heparin; the heart valves, which are used as replacements in human surgery; and even the pig's skin, which can be used in the treatment of severe burns.

- ✚ *Good for anaemia, stress, and other nervous disorders.*
- ✚ *Useful for PMS and male fertility.*
- ✚ *Best eaten thoroughly cooked, with no traces of pink in the middle and with clear running juices.*
- ➖ *Some of the chemicals used in producing ham and bacon are known to be carcinogenic if consumed in excess.*
- ➖ *Bacon and ham are very high in salt and are best avoided by anyone with high blood pressure.*

## ORGAN MEAT

❸ ❹ ❺ ❾

LAMB, OX, AND PIG KIDNEYS
*Energy per 3¹/₂oz/100g 86–91 calories*

CALF, CHICKEN, LAMB, AND OX LIVER
*Energy per 3¹/₂oz/100g 92–155 calories*
*Rich in vitamins A and B, iron, and zinc*

Some people are a bit squeamish when it comes to eating organ meat, which is known in Britain as offal. On the whole this is a pity, because organ meats are delicious as well as being extremely rich sources of some nutrients. They can be high in cholesterol and many people confuse health problems associated with cholesterol-rich foods with blood cholesterol levels, but unless you have very high cholesterol levels it is perfectly safe to enjoy both liver and kidneys from time to time.

Kidneys are extremely rich sources of vitamin $B_{12}$—3¹/₂oz/100g supplies 40 times more than you need for a day. They also have a high content of biotin, folic acid, and a significant amount of vitamin C. Liver is a major source of easily absorbed iron (essential for blood formation) and zinc (vital for healthy sperm and potency). A lack of zinc is one of the common causes of exhaustion and poor appetite. Liver also contains a huge amount of vitamin A, lots of the

B vitamins (especially $B_{12}$), and significant amounts of vitamin C. Ox liver contains the most $B_{12}$ and at one time was the medical treatment for pernicious anemia.

There are variations of nutrients between calf, chicken, lamb, ox, and pig livers, but they are all rich in the vitamin A, which is so essential for healthy skin and good night vision. Vitamin A is fat-soluble and is stored in the liver, not excreted by the body.

➕ *Good for anemia, skin and eye problems (especially for poor night vision).*

➕ *Beneficial for general fatigue, male fertility and potency.*

➕ *Best eaten in stews or casseroles (lamb, ox, or pig liver), or lightly sautéed (calf liver, chicken liver, or kidneys).*

➖ *Pregnant women, or those who are attempting to get pregnant, should not eat liver, liver pâté, or liver sausage.*

# POULTRY

*Prized for its protein, vitamin B, and mineral content*

Between the 1960s and the 1990s poultry consumption rose in almost every country, with a worldwide average increase of 50 percent. This was almost entirely due to the increased risk of coronary heart disease associated with diets that are high in saturated fats—with a large amount of that fat coming from meat. Poultry contains less saturated fat, and most of it lies around the skin, so it can easily be removed. It is an excellent source of protein, iron, and zinc (though it contains less iron, weight for weight, than most red meat), as well as a useful source of B vitamins. While chicken in particular requires careful cooking, all poultry offers a succulent and nutritious feast.

QUAIL

However, increased consumption has led to more intensive rearing of poultry, resulting generally in meat with less flavor, more saturated fat, and unwanted hormones and antibiotics.

Since chicken and turkey have moved from being a luxury item for a Sunday dinner, or a Thanksgiving and Christmas treat, to the realms of the everyday, there is now almost an infinite variety of ways in which to prepare poultry. In casseroles, stir-fries, wonderful warming soup, or used cold for sandwiches or salads, chicken and turkey are likely to continue to provide a highly nutritious part of our diet, while their fattier—but equally delicious—cousins, duck and goose, remain an occasional treat to be savored on more special occasions.

TURKEY

## CHICKEN

❶ ❺ ❾

*Energy per 3¹/₂ oz / 100g 153 calories*
*Rich in protein, iron, and zinc*

Until the advent of intensively reared poultry, chicken and turkey were luxury meats. They are now so cheap that they are everyday foods for most people, but the price we pay is lack of flavor and texture, a higher saturated fat content, and the risk of unwanted chemical residues.

Chicken meat contains far less fat than other red meats and, as most of this is contained in the skin, it is easily removed. As well as protein, chicken provides easily absorbed iron and zinc (twice as much in the dark meat as in the breast), making it an excellent food during pregnancy and beneficial as a blood- and resistance-builder. Chicken breast contains double the dark meat's quantity of vitamin B₆, so it is useful for PMS.

➕ *Good for convalescence, anemia, and for building general resistance.*
➕ *Beneficial for PMS and pregnancy (free-range and organic only).*
➕ *Best eaten broiled, roasted, barbecued, hot or cold—all without skin; excellent as soup.*
➖ *Undercooked chicken is a common cause of food poisoning.*

## DUCK

❶ ❺ ❾

*Energy per standard portion*
*361 calories*
*Rich in protein, iron, and zinc*

Duck is also an excellent source of protein, iron, zinc, and nearly all the B vitamins. Delicious though the crispy skin is, you will get 1oz/29g of fat if you eat 3¹/₂oz/100g of meat and skin, but only ¹/₄oz/ 9.7g if you stick to the meat.

It is important to cook duck on a rack, so that all the fat it contains drips into the bottom of the pan—but don't cook the potatoes there. It also helps to prick the skin all over with a sharp fork or skewer so that the fat layer under the skin can trickle out as it melts.

Served with traditional apple sauce, duck not only tastes wonderful, but the pectins in the apple help the body to eliminate much of the cholesterol eaten with the duck.

➕ *Valuable for PMS and for pregnancy (free-range and organic poultry only).*
➕ *Useful for convalescence, anemia, and for building general resistance.*
➕ *Best eaten broiled, roasted, barbecued, hot or cold—all without skin.*

## GOOSE

❶ ❺ ❾

*Energy per 3¹/₂ oz / 100g 319 calories*
*Rich in iron, zinc, and vitamin B₁₂*

Goose is enormously fatty, containing almost as much fat as protein, although this is easily reduced by placing the bird on a rack over a large pan of water, then covering the bird in tin foil and tucking the edges of the foil inside the pan. Heat on top of the stove until the water boils, then let the goose steam for half an hour. Discard the fat-laden water, then roast the goose on the rack as normal, deducting half an hour from the cooking time. When cooked, don't eat the skin.

Goose is tremendously rich in iron and zinc, makes a good source of phosphorus and potassium, and 3¹/₂ oz/100g of goose will provide more than a day's recommended dose of vitamin B₁₂.

➕ *Useful for PMS and for pregnancy (free-range and organic poultry only).*
➕ *Beneficial for convalescence, anemia, and for building general resistance.*
➕ *Best eaten broiled, roasted, barbecued, hot or cold—all without skin.*

## TURKEY

❶ ❺ ❾

*Energy per 3¹/₂oz / 100g 319 calories*
*Rich in protein, iron, and zinc*

Unlike other poultry, turkey is extremely low in fat, containing only 2.7g per 3¹/₂oz/100g. It is rich in protein and supplies easily absorbed iron and zinc (more in the dark meat than in the white). But its low fat content tends to make it a dry, insipid bird unless great care is taken when cooking it. Generally speaking, the larger the bird, the better the flavor. You can even enjoy some of the skin as a crispy treat.

➕ *Good for convalescence, anemia, and for building general resistance.*
➕ *Beneficial for PMS and for pregnancy (free-range and organic poultry only).*
➕ *Best eaten grilled, roasted, barbecued, hot or cold; excellent as soup.*

### SUPER FOOD

● All poultry can be used to make soup, though it is important to remove as much fat as possible. The protein content of such soup is very easily absorbed, making it good for invalids, a poor immune system, chronic fatigue, and sexual dysfunction.

# GAME AND GAME BIRDS

*Prized for their protein and mineral content*

There is now a growing interest in the consumption of game—both feathered and furred—and the deep, full flavors of a crisply roasted pheasant, a venison hotpot, a wild turkey, a wood pigeon, or a game pie exemplify the greatest traditions of English and American cooking. According to John Ash and Sid Goldstein in their wonderful book, **American Game Cooking**, *the farmed game of America is the perfect compromise. The animals range freely over huge areas without restraint, are raised without artificial growth hormones, antibiotics, or steroids, and are inspected for quality, health, and lack of parasites.*

Most game is high in protein and low in fat compared with other meats. Game birds also provide considerably more potassium, calcium, phosphorus, iron, thiamin, vitamin $B_6$, $B_{12}$, and folate than other meats.

The best way to cook all young game birds is to roast them with a slice of bacon placed over the breast. A hot oven gives a crispy brown skin, but game should never be overcooked. Older game birds are best served as a casserole. Do be aware, when preparing game, that in some cases the lead shot may still be present, and ensure you take the utmost care to remove the pellets before cooking.

## GROUSE
**❶ ❺**

*Energy per 3¹/₂oz/100g 59 calories*
*Rich in protein, iron, and B vitamins*

Almost impossible to rear commercially, the British red grouse is highly prized by Scottish grouse-moor shooters and by the diners in restaurants throughout Britain, which compete to offer the first grouse of the season after the "glorious twelfth." Allow one bird per person.

## PARTRIDGE
**❶ ❺**

*Energy per 3¹/₂oz/100g 127 calories*
*Rich in protein, iron, and vitamins*

Succulent and strongly flavored, wild partridge have much less fat than farmed birds, so they need extra lard and frequent basting. Partridge and grouse both make wonderfully delicious casseroles. Allow one average bird per person.

## QUAIL
**❶ ❺**

*Energy per 3¹/₂oz/100g 100 calories*
*Rich in protein, iron, and vitamins*

One of the smallest and most delicately flavored of game birds. Allow two per person and roast them with herbs, broil, or even barbecue them. The only way to eat quail is by using your fingers.

## PHEASANT
**❶ ❺**

*Energy per 3¹/₂oz/100g 114 calories*
*Rich in protein, iron, and vitamins*

Shot pheasant is usually allowed to hang for several days, producing a stronger, gamey flavor. Supermarket birds are normally not hung, so they are generally not as gamey. An average pheasant serves two people.

## PIGEON
❶ ❺

*Energy per 3¹/₂oz / 100g 88 calories*
*Rich in protein, iron, and vitamins*

The English wood pigeon is a very lean bird, and only wild ones are available. They roast well, but the best part is the breast, which can often be found smoked and thinly sliced.

The American equivalent, squab, is commercially raised and contains a small amount of fat. It is slightly larger than the wild pigeon and should be roasted quickly and never overcooked. It is delicious deboned and either sautéed or broiled with fresh thyme.

✚ *Extremely low in saturated fat.*
✚ *Best eaten roasted in a hot oven; older birds can be casseroled.*

## RABBIT
❶ ❺

*Energy per 3¹/₂oz / 100g 68 calories*
*Rich in protein*

Farmed or wild, rabbit makes a delicious and delicately flavored dish—high in protein, low in fat, and, in terms of calories/weight ratio, it contains the fewest calories of all. Joints of rabbit can be broiled or sautéed, but rabbit stew is the traditional and best method of cooking. The wild hare, or the jackrabbit, as it is known in the United States, is more difficult to come by, although its numbers have increased in recent years. It is fine when marinated and roasted while young, but otherwise wild hare can be a bit on the tough side and for this reason is best served in a stew.

To compensate for the rabbit's lack of many nutrients, except for protein, use plenty of root vegetables in the stew and serve with a large salad.

✚ *Extremely low in saturated fat.*
✚ *Best eaten casseroled.*

## VENISON
❶ ❺

*Energy per 3¹/₂oz / 100g 165 calories*
*Rich in protein*

Though usually farmed rather than wild, venison is now making a comeback. When properly dressed and hung, the flavors and texture are superb. Delivering only one-third of the calories and half the fat of beef, and considerably less than chicken, venison is a healthy option. Prime cuts should be cooked at a very hot temperature and for just enough time to be medium-rare. Otherwise, marinate the venison before cooking. Red wine, oil, and herbs are common marinades in Europe, while buttermilk is a favorite in the United States.

English venison hotpot with vegetables and the American hunter's campfire recipe cooked in coffee and cider vinegar are both wonderful.

✚ *Extremely low in saturated fat.*
✚ *Best eaten cooked in a hot oven or marinated, then casseroled.*

## WILD TURKEY
❶ ❺

*Energy per 3¹/₂oz / 100g 114 calories*
*Rich in protein, iron, and zinc*

The traditional wild turkey of North America bears little resemblance to the white-fleshed variety eaten in the millions on Christmas Day. Wild turkey has a wonderful flavor, a firm texture, and very little fat, as well as being rich in protein, iron, and zinc. You can roast your bird in the same way as its domestic cousin.

John Ash and Sid Goldstein have several traditional recipes in their cookbook, *American Game Cooking*, and my favorite combines the American wild turkey with onions, spices, chilies, and that other great Mexican contribution to food—chocolate—resulting in Turkey Molé.

✚ *Extremely low in saturated fat.*
✚ *Best eaten broiled, roasted, barbecued, hot or cold.*

# FISH AND SHELLFISH

*Prized for their protein and mineral content*

SHRIMP

*A*lthough we have moved on a long way from the days of hunter-gathering, fish is the one component of our diet that is still largely hunted.

Since the beginning of the 1960s the fish-processing industry has accounted for a considerable proportion of the fish that we eat, much of it in the form of fish sticks, pre-prepared supermarket dishes, and canned fish. Unfortunately, it appears that many home cooks are afraid of fish, being unsure how to prepare and cook it and how long it will keep. Fresh fish is indeed highly perishable (especially the oily fish), but common sense is all that is needed, and good health dictates that we should be eating far more than we do.

Fish remains an exceptional source of protein and minerals, and saltwater fish are particularly valuable for their high iodine content. B vitamins are found in all types of fish, and oily fish are valuable sources of vitamins A, D, and E, together with the omega-3 essential fatty acids.

The best ways to cook fish are baking, steaming, broiling, or pan-frying in shallow oil, because all these methods minimize the loss of nutrients. Watch out, though, for additives in any processed fish that you buy.

SARDINES

SARDINES

HERRING

## OILY FISH

**② ③ ④ ⑥**

HERRING
*Energy per standard portion 171 calories*

TUNA (CANNED)
*Energy per standard portion 85 calories*
*Rich in protein, calcium, and vitamin D*

Mackerel, salmon, trout, tuna, herrings, anchovy, sardine, smelt, sprats, and eels are now known to contain high levels of eicosapentanoeic acid, one of a group of fatty acids belonging to the omega-3 family, which are essential to healthy cell function. A number of studies have demonstrated their value in such diverse conditions as atherosclerosis, arthritis, and rheumatoid arthritis, cyclic breast pain, and skin diseases like eczema and psoriasis.

As well as being exceptionally rich in vitamin D (3½oz/100g of grilled fresh herring or canned salmon, or a broiled bloater, supplies more than a week's worth), small oily fish—like sprats, smelt, and canned sardines— are excellent sources of calcium. Canned tuna, however, contains less than half the vitamin D of fresh tuna, the rest being lost during the processing stage.

As well as the fat-soluble vitamins, oily fish provide energy and minerals—sprats supply the same quantity of iron, weight for weight, as beef; sardines the same as lamb.

When buying fish canned in oil, choose those canned in olive, sunflower, or soybean oil. Drain off all surplus oil before consumption.

- ➕ *Contain essential fatty acids as well as a powerhouse of vitamins and minerals.*
- ➕ *Good for almost everyone (except for those with allergies or gout).*
- ➕ *Useful for weight control.*
- ➕ *Beneficial for rheumatism, osteoarthritis, rheumatoid arthritis, eczema, psoriasis, cyclic breast pain, and most inflammatory diseases.*
- ➕ *Useful for heart protection.*
- ➕ *Best eaten baked, steamed, broiled, or pan-fried.*
- ➖ *Eating large amounts of smoked food has been linked to a higher incidence of cancer, so smoked fish should be occasional treats.*
- ➖ *Gout sufferers should avoid herring and its roe, anchovies, smelt, sardines, salmon, sprats, mackerel.*

PLAICE

# WHITE FISH

✷ ✷

PLAICE

*Energy per 3¹/₂oz / 100g 79 calories*
*Rich in protein and B vitamins*

All white fish are all very similar from a nutritional standpoint, whether they are saltwater fish—like cod, haddock, whiting, monkfish, sea bream, catfish, red and gray mullet, snappers, plaice, sole, and halibut—or freshwater fish, like pike, perch, bream, and carp. They contain virtually no fat, few calories, and plenty of protein. They all contain B vitamins but little iron, and although halibut (which is slightly oily) may contribute a little vitamin A, white fish do not in general supply fat-soluble vitamins. Cod and halibut liver are very rich in vitamins A, D, and E, but these are used solely for the production of oil. White fish roe is an excellent source of B vitamins and as good a source of iron as some meat. Fish roe contains cholesterol, so it may pose a health risk for people suffering from high blood-cholesterol.

There is no disputing the health benefits of consuming less red meat, and what better substitute than lots more fish? The World Health Organization's food pyramid advises eating fish a few times each week.

➕ *Contain a powerhouse of vitamins and minerals not easily obtained from other food sources.*

➕ *Beneficial for weight control.*

➕ *Useful for heart protection.*

➕ *Good for almost everyone (except for those with allergies or gout).*

➕ *Best eaten baked, steamed, broiled, or pan-fried.*

➖ *Gout sufferers should avoid cod, caviar, and taramasalata.*

## BUYING FISH

● When buying fish, check that the eyes look bright and shiny; that the skin still has lots of scales on; and that the gills are red. Fish should always have the fresh smell of the sea. Look for well-defined markings.

● Shellfish should feel heavy for their size. All mollusks should be closed, and all shellfish should be eaten on the day you buy it.

## SHELLFISH

❷ ❹ ❾

OYSTERS
*Energy per standard portion 78 calories*

SHRIMP
*Energy per standard portion 59 calories*
*Rich in protein, iron and zinc*

Shellfish can be divided conveniently into crustaceans—crabs, lobsters, prawns, shrimps, crayfish, spiny lobster—and mollusks—mussels, oysters, cockles, whelks, winkles, clams, and scallops. All shellfish contain the same amount of protein and other nutrients as white fish, although they are much saltier, while mollusks contain far more iron and vitamin A. They are also excellent sources of zinc, especially oysters, cockles, whelks, and winkles.

### SUPER FOOD

● Casanova knew a thing or to. The greatest lover of all time used to eat 70 oysters a day, which he claimed were the reason for his super-stud performance. It is now known that they contain large quantities of zinc—essential for the production of sperm and the maintenance of male potency. A dozen oysters provide enough zinc for a whole week.

There has been a lot of controversy about the high cholesterol content of some shellfish, but most experts now agree that this is a hazard only for those suffering from genetic lipid-metabolism diseases. A regular intake of shellfish has been shown to reduce the level of the LDL fats that are most dangerous to the heart. Shellfish also contain small amounts of the cardio-protective essential omega-3 fatty acids.

Another good reason for eating shellfish is their high selenium content. Selenium deficiency has been closely linked with heart disease and a greater risk of cancer of the esophagus and prostate.

➕ *Beneficial for weight control.*
➕ *Useful for heart protection.*
➕ *Best eaten on the day of purchase.*
➖ *Gout sufferers should avoid scallops and mussels.*
➖ *Shellfish are a fairly common cause of severe food allergy.*

# STARCHY FOODS

*Bread and yeast*

*Cereals*

*Pasta*

*Rice*

# STARCHY FOODS

The major foods in this group, which are referred to as starchy or complex carbohydrate foods, are the cereals (grains) wheat, rice, corn (maize), millet, sorghum, barley, oats, and rye, and products made from them, such as bread, pasta, and breakfast cereals. They are staples in most diets worldwide, with rice being the main cereal eaten, followed by wheat and corn.

Generally, in the developing world, cereals (and other starchy foods) already make up the largest part of dietary volume and energy, whereas in the developed world current dietary recommendations encourage us to choose more plant-based foods and aim to obtain 55–60 percent of our dietary energy from starchy foods. Interestingly, as societies become more industrialized, cereals supply less of the total energy, and cereal and cereal products become more refined and processed in other ways.

Cereals contain an average of 70 percent starch by weight. They also provide varying amounts of dietary fiber, protein, B vitamins, vitamin E, and various trace elements. Their nutrient content is greatly affected by the ways in which they are processed. Most of the nonstarch nutrients are concentrated in the germ and husks of cereals, which are

WHOLEWHEAT BREAD

often removed during processing. The more refined a cereal product is, the fewer vitamins, minerals, and fiber it

PUMPERNICKEL

will contain, so cereals should always be eaten in wholegrain form, or in a less processed form, such as wholegrain bread, brown rice, or pasta. Keeping to a minimum in your diet the highly sweetened and processed breakfast cereals, and baked goods such as cookies and cakes—which generally contain substantial amounts of fat, sugar, and salt—is a challenge worth pursuing. They are heavily marketed, while the wide variety of healthier wholegrains in different forms is never given the same emphasis.

Starchy foods are mistakenly still thought to be fattening foods. This myth should be exploded, since the main constituent of cereals and their products is starch— which gram for gram supplies a quarter of the energy (calories) of fat, at the same time providing protein and valuable amounts of vitamins and minerals.

SPAGHETTI

The main contributors to the calories associated with starchy foods are the high-fat sauces, or the fats and other spreads, often served with them.

FRENCH STICK

## BREAD

② ⑤

BROWN BREAD
*Energy per standard portion 78 calories*

WHITE BREAD
*Energy per standard portion 85 calories*

WHOLEWHEAT BREAD
*Energy per standard portion 77 calories*
*Rich in fiber, iron, and vitamins*

Good bread really is "the staff of life" but, in spite of all the evidence to the contrary, most people still believe that bread is fattening. In fact, bread is a vital part of a healthy, balanced diet, and can be an aid to weight loss.

The first thing to understand is the difference between complex and refined carbohydrates. Refined carbohydrates are those such as sugars and highly processed starches, which provide large quantities of empty calories. Complex carbohydrates are found in wholegrain cereals such as brown rice, pasta, oats, barley, and wholegrain wheat. These supply many other essential nutrients, and are also a rich source of vital fiber. All of the "good" complex carbohydrates help to fill you up, and displace the high-fat, high-sugar foods that are every slimmer's enemy.

While white bread is not in itself bad for you, not eating wholewheat bread is unhealthy. Six slices of wholewheat bread each day will supply just over half of the total amount of fiber that you should consume and a good proportion of the minimum 50 percent of your calories that should come from complex carbohydrates. Wholewheat bread also contains significant amounts of vitamin E, which is not present at all in white bread; more potassium, iron, zinc, copper, magnesium, thiamin, riboflavin, pantothenic acid, folic acid, pyridoxine, and biotin. It provides ten times as much manganese as white bread, twice as much chromium, and one-and-a-half times as much selenium.

However, you should not rely on wholewheat bread as being a good dietary source of calcium, magnesium, or zinc, since it contains much more of the chemical phytic acid than white bread, which interferes with the body's absorption of these particular minerals. ▶

WHOLEWHEAT BREAD

SODA BREAD

**bread continued**

If your diet includes plenty of wholewheat bread, then you can also eat some of the more exotic breads as well without a guilty conscience. If children don't seem eager to eat wholewheat bread, try making sandwiches with one slice of wholewheat and one of white. Do avoid the so-called "starch-reduced" varieties of bread, which contain around 80 percent more calories in the same weight of bread. And some white loaves specially made for toasting contain added sugar, so that they go a pleasing golden brown under the broiler.

Nowhere are the influences of other cultures more obvious than in the breads they produce—using different processes, different mixtures of grains, with and without yeast, with the addition of herbs, spices, and toppings. But the key to getting the best out of your daily bread is what you put on it: a thick layer of butter or a large dollop of jam will do more harm than good.

➕ *Good for weight loss and stress.*

➕ *A useful source of healthy calories for the physically active.*

➕ *Beneficial for constipation, diverticulitis, and piles.*

➕ *Best eaten as wholewheat bread—either fresh or toasted.*

➖ *Watch out for the amount of salt in commercially produced bread. The label that says "530mg of sodium per 100g of bread" actually means that $3^{1}/_{2}oz/100g$ of bread has a salt content of 1.3g—more than a quarter of the total recommended salt intake per day.*

➖ *People suffering from celiac disease are not able to eat food containing gluten; conventional bread can make them extremely ill and must be avoided.*

### FAST FOOD FACT

● **A bread poultice is the best way to draw an erupting boil. Put some slices of bread in a sieve and pour boiling water over them. Use a wooden spoon to stir the bread around until it forms a moist hot ball. Turn out into a clean cloth and squeeze out the surplus moisture. When cool enough for comfort, apply the poultice to the affected area and leave until it gets cold. Repeat until the boil comes to a head and bursts. Keep it covered with a sterile dressing until the skin has healed.**

## BREAD FACTS

What follows is a nutritional comparison of some of the most popular types of bread (quoted per 3½oz/100g of bread).

| Type of bread | calories | fiber in grams |
|---|---|---|
| WHITE BREAD: refined flour with a host of additives. Often fortified with vitamins and minerals, including calcium. | 235 | 1.5 |
| BROWN BREAD: sometimes white-flour colored, but may contain some less refined flour. May be fortified like white bread. | 218 | 3.5 |
| WHOLEWHEAT BREAD: made from 100 percent flour with all the bran, fiber, and vitamins. Contains more of almost everything, especially vitamins B and E, iron, zinc, and selenium. | 215 | 5.8 |
| CHAPATI: classic Indian bread. | 328 | 2.5 |
| FRENCH BREAD: delicious with cheese or salami, but low in fiber, high in salt, with a bonus of high iron. | 270 | 1.5 |
| GRANARY: better than brown bread, because made with malt flour and whole wheat kernels—mind your teeth. | 235 | 4.3 |
| MATZOS: traditional Jewish unleavened bread, eaten to celebrate Passover, but now available all year round. Virtually salt-free (about 5 percent in other breads). | 384 | 3.0 |
| MILK BREAD: higher in calcium, but also fat. | 296 | 1.9 |
| NAAN: another traditional Indian bread. | 336 | 1.9 |
| PITA, WHOLEWHEAT: traditional Greek bread with less salt, more fiber, iron, and zinc. | 265 | 5.2 |
| PUMPERNICKEL: traditional German bread made from a mixture of wholegrains, including rye. Valuable for its low-fat, high-fiber content, vitamin E, and iron. | 219 | 7.5 |
| RYE BREAD: another traditional European bread, which is high in fiber, low in fat, high in vitamin E, and a good source of iron and zinc. | 219 | 4.4 |
| SODA BREAD: traditional nonyeast bread from the remote parts of Scotland, Wales, and Ireland. Originally made with bicarbonate of soda and cream of tartar, and cooked on a bakestone. | 258 | 2.1 |

## YEAST

⑤

DRIED YEAST
*Energy per 3¹/₂oz / 100g 169 calories*
*Rich in B vitamins and folic acid*

Yeast, as used in baking and brewing, has been a friend to humanity since time immemorial, but in recent years it has been getting a bad press. There are many strains of yeast, but only one actually causes health problems in humans—*Candida albicans*, the yeast present in the gut and mouth that is responsible for thrush. Oral and vaginal thrush are probably the most common infections, followed by skin infections and anal thrush in babies, as a sequel to severe diaper rash.

In general terms, severe infections with *Candida* are seen in the very young, the elderly, as a result of antibiotic treatment, and frequently in patients whose immune system is compromised by disease (HIV), chemotherapy, radiotherapy, or by the long-term use of some drugs, most particularly corticosteroids and oral contraceptives.

There is a general acceptance that reducing sugar consumption helps in the treatment of proven *Candida* infections, but the concept of systemic candidiasis—popularly believed in the field of complementary medicine to be responsible for a number of vaguely defined, multiple-symptom illnesses such as chronic fatigue and multiple allergies, and widely discussed in the media—has not been generally accepted by the medical profession. Anyone—and particularly children— prescribed a rigid dietary program excluding foods that have a link with any form of yeast would be well advised to consult a qualified medical practitioner working in the field.

- ➕ *Baker's and brewer's yeast are good sources of B vitamins and folic acid.*
- ➕ *Good for maintaining the nervous system and for healthy metabolism.*
- ➖ *A very small percentage of people are yeast-sensitive and need to avoid yeast-containing foods.*

# CEREALS

*Prized for their starch content*

Cereal is the name given to the seeds of a group of plants from the grass family. The most important cereals grown throughout the world are barley, corn, millet, oats, rice, rye, and wheat. Their nutritional value is much the same and their main constituent is starch. But all cereals are only as nutritious as the soil in which they grow, and those that have been grown in selenium-poor soil may give rise to a deficiency in this vital mineral.

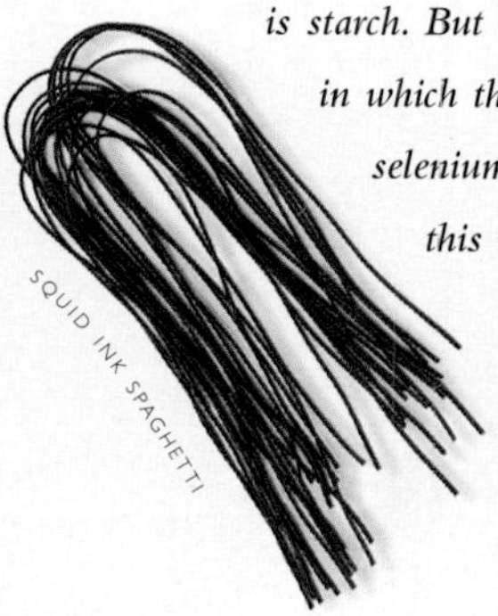

SQUID INK SPAGHETTI

All of the unrefined wholegrain cereals are richer in fiber, B vitamins, and minerals than refined cereals. With the exception of yellow corn, none of them provides beta-carotene. Cereals also lack vitamins C and $B_{12}$, so that in spite of their being the staple food for many indigenous populations, unless they are combined with other vegetables and some animal protein sources, deficiency diseases follow.

People suffering from celiac disease should avoid wheat flour, barley, oats, and rye, all of which contain gluten, which can cause them serious malabsorption problems and illness.

Sago, tapioca, and arrowroot are frequently called cereals, but they are not seeds, so they do not contain the germ layer that is rich in B vitamins, and they are also very low in protein.

WHEAT

## BARLEY

① ② ④ ⑤ ⑧

*Energy per standard portion 72 calories*
*Rich in soluble fiber and B-complex vitamins*

The botanical name for barley is *Hordeum* and in Roman times it was so highly thought of as a strengthening food that some of the greatest gladiators were called *Hordearii*, since barley was their staple food. All forms of barley contain soluble fiber and beta glucans, which help the body to get rid of excess cholesterol. They also contain some of the protease inhibitors, which have a definite cancer-protective action.

Now is your chance to benefit from this wonderful grain. Use lots of barley in your cooking: as flour added to recipes for cookies, muffins, and cakes; as grits in cereal and vegetable mixtures; boiled in water to make drinks; and added to soups. It makes milk more easily digestible, especially for babies, and is good baked with milk to make puddings.

Herbalists have traditionally used lemon barley water for the treatment of cystitis and all other urinary infections. To make your own, put ½oz/15g of washed pot barley in a pan with 2½ cups/500ml of water and two washed, quartered, unwaxed lemons. Bring to a boil, cover, and simmer gently for 30 minutes. Strain, keep in the refrigerator and drink several glasses a day.

⊕ *Beneficial for urinary infections and for constipation.*

⊕ *Good for inflammations of the throat, esophagus, and digestive tract.*

⊕ *Helps lower cholesterol levels and protect against cancer.*

⊕ *Best eaten as pot barley (more nutritious than pearl barley).*

⊖ *Not suitable for those suffering from celiac disease.*

### SUPER FOOD

● The soothing demulcents in barley make it an ideal food for the relief of sore throats, esophagitis, gastritis, and colitis and, like other grains, barley is mineral-rich.

Containing calcium, potassium, and plenty of the B-complex vitamins, barley is useful for people suffering from stress or fatigue, and a nourishing food for convalescents.

## BUCKWHEAT

*Energy per standard portion 73 calories*
*Rich in rutin*

This cereal was either brought to Europe from Asia by the Crusaders or to Spain by the Arabs some centuries before.

Although it is popularly considered a grain, buckwheat is in reality a seed, rich in the flavonoid glycoside known as rutin. This strengthens and tones the walls of the tiniest blood vessels, the capillaries, making buckwheat useful in cases of frostbite or chilblains, as well as for capillary fragility in general. It is also recommended by herbalists for treating varicose veins. Rutin is a great aid in the treatment of high blood pressure and hardening of the arteries.

Buckwheat flour makes delicious and nourishing pancakes and is widely used in Oriental cooking. But for a real flavor treat, combined with good nutrition, it is hard to beat the traditional Russian pancakes known as *blinis*—delicious, especially eaten with lemon tea.

➕ *Beneficial for the circulation and high blood pressure.*
➕ *Best eaten as pancakes.*

## BULGAR

*Energy per standard portion*
*353 calories*
*Rich in protein, niacin, and iron*

In the Middle East cracked wheat is often used instead of rice. It is made by soaking whole wheat grains in water, then putting them into a very hot oven until they crack. These nutty-flavored grains make a great addition to salads and are particularly good as the Lebanese recipe, tabbouleh.

➖ *Not suitable for those suffering from celiac disease.*

## COUSCOUS

*Energy per 3¹/₂oz / 100g 227 calories*
*Rich in starch and niacin*

This is one of the most popular dishes from North Africa. It is prepared from the inner part of the wheat grain and can be used for sweet or savory dishes.

## CORN

②

FLOUR
*Energy per 3¹/₂oz / 100g 353 calories*

GRITS
*Energy per 3¹/₂oz / 100g 262 calories*

CORNSTARCH
*Energy per 3¹/₂oz / 100g 354 calories*
*Rich in starch and potassium*

Originally native to South America, corn, or maize, has become a staple food in many poor areas of the world. It is not so long ago that the deficiency disease pellagra was common in the southern American states, where corn made up the bulk of food for poor communities. Pellagra causes itchy, scaly red skin, sores in the mouth, brain lesions, damage to the nervous system, and difficulty in walking.

Ground corn and popcorn provide the nutrients from the whole grain, while grits are made from milled corn and lose nutrients, like white flour. Cornstarch, made from the pulverized grain, is used in baking and for thickening sauces. The Italians use corn to make polenta, and in Mexico it is used to make tortillas.

✚ *Valuable for celiacs, since it is gluten-free.*
✚ *Best used to make porridgelike dishes such as polenta or in baking.*

## MILLET

② ③

*Energy per 3¹/₂cz / 100g 282 calories*
*Rich in protein and silicon*

Millet is another cereal suitable for sufferers of celiac disease because it contains no gluten. It is highly regarded by naturopaths, and the American natural healer Paavo Airola describes it as "the most nutritious cereal in the world—a truly wonderful complete food, high in protein and low in starches—very easily digested and never causes gas and fermentation in the stomach."

Millet is rich in silicon, which is vital for the health of hair, skin, teeth, eyes, and nails. Lack of this mineral can result in a sagging of the body's connective tissue. And, because millet is never highly refined, it retains all its essential nutrients. The best-known variety of millet is sorghum. This much-ignored cereal in the United States and Britain, although popular with "food reformers," should be used much more widely.

✚ *Valuable for celiacs, since it is gluten-free.*
✚ *Good for the skin, hair, nails, teeth, and eyes.*
✚ *Best used in salads, as a thickener in soups and stews, or to make bread.*

## OATS
❹

*Energy per 3¹/₂oz / 100g 401 calories*
*Rich in calcium, potassium,*
*and magnesium*

Oats have played an important part in traditional herbal practice: possets and caudles made from oatmeal have long been a standard remedy. Oats are richly nutritious, containing over 12g of protein in 3½oz/100g of oats; also polyunsaturated fats, a little vitamin E, and plenty of the B-complex vitamins. They are also spectacularly high in calcium, potassium, and magnesium.

Dr. James Anderson of the Veterans' Administration Hospital in Kentucky has shown that the cholesterol levels of patients fed a daily dose of oat bran have declined. And research into the benefits of the soluble fiber in oats has finally persuaded the Food and Drug Administration (FDA) to take the unprecedented step of approving a food-specific health claim for them.

➕ *Beneficial for lowering blood cholesterol.*
➕ *Best eaten as porridge, as oat bran, or used in baking.*
➖ *Not suitable for celiacs.*

## RYE
❸ ❺

*Energy per 3¹/₂oz / 100g 379 calories*
*Rich in fiber, B vitamins,*
*and zinc*

The nutritional value of rye is similar to that of wheat, with two important exceptions. It contains considerably more fiber and far less gluten, so rye bread does not rise a great deal and tends to be much heavier than wheat bread, but for people who do not have celiac disease but have an adverse reaction to gluten, rye is often well tolerated. Rye grows well in cold climates, so rye breads are popular in Scandinavia, Russia, and northern Germany.

Most rye breads are a mixture of rye and wheat flours, but pumpernickel and black bread should be made exclusively from rye. If you have gluten problems, check the labels carefully—it is quite common for rye breads to be colored with caramel to make them darker, so you can't judge by the color alone.

➕ *May be tolerated by those with a gluten reaction.*
➕ *Best eaten as bread or crispbread.*
➖ *Not suitable for those suffering from celiac disease.*

## SEMOLINA

❷ ❸ ❹ ❾

*Energy per standard portion 70 calories*
*Rich in starch*
*and protein*

Semolina is produced by extracting the coarse particles of the wheat endosperm, which are sifted and then separated. In India and the Middle East it is used to make wonderful sweet desserts, which are often flavored with rose water or other perfumed extracts. In Italy it forms the basic ingredient of that wonderful dish, gnocchi, which is prepared with milk, semolina, egg, Parmesan, and nutmeg—a rich and delicious combination of essential nutrients. In the United States semolina is a popular hot breakfast cereal.

➕ *Easily digested, so valuable*
  *for convalescents.*
➕ *Best eaten as a dessert, a hot*
  *breakfast cereal, or as gnocchi.*
➖ *Not suitable for those suffering*
  *from celiac disease.*

## WHEAT

❷ ❺

*Energy per 3½oz / 100g 386 calories*
*Rich in B-complex vitamins*
*and vitamin E*

This cereal is a vitally important staple food n the Western diet—the majority of wheat ending up as flour and finally as bread. Although refined wheat flour is fortified with some of the nutrients that are lost in the manufacturing process, zinc, magnesium, vitamin $B_6$, pyridoxine, vitamin E, and fiber are not replaced. The wheat germ left over when white flour is made is a rich source of the B-complex vitamins and vitamin E. It is rich in unsaturated fatty acids and an excellent food supplement. Sprouted wheat is also very rich in nutrients.

A centuries-old British dish called frumenty—whole wheat grains baked overnight in the ashes of the fire to burst open and set into a thick jelly—was the perfect meal for millions of farm laborers in years gone by.

➕ *Beneficial for invalids and*
  *convalescents.*
➕ *Best used in baking, in making*
  *pasta, or as wheat germ added*
  *to cereals.*
➖ *Not suitable for those suffering*
  *from celiac disease.*

CORNFLAKES

BRAN FLAKES

MUESLI

## BREAKFAST CEREALS

❷ ❹ ❽

CORNFLAKES
*Energy per standard portion 108 calories*

MUESLI
*Energy per standard portion 184 calories*

PORRIDGE
*Energy per standard portion 133 calories*
*Rich in soluble and insoluble fiber and B vitamins*

You might think that these early-morning foods are a product of the late twentieth century, but archaeologists have found evidence of oats being used by the ancient Greeks and Romans.

In the United States, the history of breakfast cereals is inextricably linked with the famous health pioneer Dr. John Kellogg and with his sanatorium at Battle Creek, Michigan. He is best known for inventing cornflakes in 1899, but was also responsible for inventing "granola," which he developed during the 1860s. Together with Shredded Wheat and Weetabix (the only cereal actually invented in England), these variations on natural cereals were developed as "health foods," which, with the addition of milk, provide a highly nutritious start to the day. Most modern commercial breakfast cereals, however, contain large amounts of added sugar, and sometimes salt. Products aimed at the children's market tend to be by far the worst in nutritional terms, some being 50 percent sugar by weight.

The majority of commercial mueslis are also a pale and nutritionally inferior substitute for the real thing, discovered by the famous Swiss physician and pioneer of the natural health movement, Dr. Max Bircher-Benner, when he shared a shepherd's supper in the Swiss mountains—a porridgelike dish common to the country peasants.

➕ *Wholegrain cereals are complex carbohydrates providing slow-release energy for several hours.*

➕ *Oats are one of the great mood-enhancing foods, and are beneficial for bowel function and cholesterol elimination.*

➕ *Best eaten fresh, with milk but no sugar.*

➖ *Many commercial brands are high in sugar and salt.*

# BRAN

OAT BRAN
*Energy per 3 1/2 oz / 100g 385 calories*

WHEAT BRAN
*Energy per 3 1/2 oz / 100g 206 calories*
*Rich in fiber*

Wheat bran is the outer husk of wheat grains and is a very rich source of dietary fiber. Oat bran contains even more soluble fiber than wheat bran. This helps to reduce cholesterol and is less irritant than insoluble fiber. Two heaped tablespoons provide the daily fiber requirement of 2/3oz/18g.

There is now no doubt that an adequate intake of fiber is essential for the proper functioning of the large bowel (colon). There is also a direct relationship between low fiber consumption, constipation, and the subsequent onset of varicose veins and hemorrhoids. The soluble form of fiber has a double benefit. First, it acts as "smoothage," rather than "roughage," speeding up the digestive process and preventing constipation. Second, it combines with cholesterol during digestion and carries it out of the body as part of the bowel function.

It is, however, far healthier to eat wholewheat bread than bran (four slices equal one tablespoon of bran).

- *Good for reducing cholesterol, for aiding digestion, and preventing constipation.*
- *Oat bran is beneficial for diabetics.*
- *Best eaten as part of a cooked product, like wholewheat bread, porridge, or muesli.*
- *Raw wheat bran in excess interferes with mineral absorption, causes flatulence, and may cause irritable bowel syndrome.*

### FAST FOOD FACT

● Bran is a wonderful remedy for skin problems. To treat eczema and psoriasis, put 4–5 tablespoons of bran onto a handkerchief-size square of cheesecloth. Gather up the four corners, twist into a neck, and tie with string. Soak the ball of bran in warm water and use like a sponge to wash the affected areas of skin; alternatively hang it under the running water as the bath fills, dissolving its beneficial substances into the bathwater.

PENNE

FARFALLE

## PASTA

②

WHITE PASTA
*Energy per standard portion 239 calories*
WHOLEWHEAT
*Energy per standard portion 226 calories*
*Rich in complex carbohydrates*

The history of pasta in Europe starts with Marco Polo, who allegedly found people eating it in China and took pasta back to his native Italy in 1295. This claim is hotly disputed by Italian foodies, who maintain that their national dish was being eaten in Italy long before Marco Polo's time. Whatever the truth, pasta, along with sun-dried fruit and vegetables, cured, smoked, and air-dried fish and meat, was among the first true convenience foods. Once made and dried, it can be kept for months and prepared in minutes, simply by boiling it in water.

Though there are many variations of pasta, there are only two basic types—the one made with flour and water and the one made with eggs—and they are very different. Traditional Italian pasta is made from nothing but flour and water, but it is the type of flour, made from durum wheat, that is so important. Known as semolina to the Italians, this flour is high in gluten and is the only flour that is suitable

to produce the best dried spaghetti and all those other wonderful pasta shapes.

Egg pasta is the kind that you can make yourself at home or, increasingly, can buy fresh in your local delicatessen or supermarket. It is made with a much softer wheat flour, with a lower gluten content, and is known to every Italian housewife as *pasta all'uovo*. In some regions, especially in the far southern areas of Apulia, olive oil and a pinch of salt are sometimes added too.

Although most pasta that is consumed is the traditional dried variety, made from white durum wheat, wholewheat pastas are now far more widely available, and are lighter and more palatable than early versions. For people with celiac disease and others who are allergic to gluten, pasta made from rice flour can also be found in specialist shops. There are also pastas available that are colored and flavored with squid ink, tomatoes, and spinach. ▶

SQUID INK SPAGHETTI

SPAGHETTI

**pasta continued**

Pasta is an excellent source of complex carbohydrates, which provide sustained, slow-release energy. Although wholewheat pasta is richer in fiber, minerals, and B vitamins, both white and wholewheat pasta are healthy foods. The idea that pasta is fattening is one of the longest-surviving food myths of the twentieth century—it is what you put on the pasta that makes it fattening. The classic *aglio e olio* (spaghetti with garlic and olive oil) or a simple mixture of extra-virgin olive oil, garlic, parsley, rosemary, thyme, and basil (*spaghetti alle erbe*), or a dish of pasta with tuna fish and scallions are all wonderful meals: satisfying, delicious, and a weight-watcher's treat.

With practice and imagination you can soon become adept at making meals in minutes. From Chinese noodles to the most exotic pasta with seafood, you can enjoy good nutrition and the mood-enhancing benefits of a high carbohydrate intake.

✚ *Good for providing energy and especially for athletes.*
✚ *Useful for convalescence.*
✚ *Beneficial for weight loss.*
✚ *Best eaten boiled until* al dente *and accompanied by a simple sauce.*

## TRADITIONAL ITALIAN PASTA

**Pasta lunga** (long pasta): all the spaghettis, spaghettinis, angel hair, linguini, fusilli, etc.
**Fettucce** (ribbons): tagliatelli, fettuccini, tagliolini, etc.
**Tubi** (tubes): all the variations of penne, macaroni, rigatoni
**Pasta shapes**: farfalle, conchiglie, orecchiette, lumache, fusilli, plus tomato-, spinach-, and various other colored pastas, such as beet and mushroom.
**Stuffed pastas**: ravioli, cappelletti, tortelloni, canneloni, lasagne, etc.

BROWN LONG-GRAIN RICE

BROWN RICE

## RICE

**② ④**

BROWN RICE
*Energy per standard portion 212 calories*

WHITE RICE
*Energy per standard portion 248 calories*
*Rich in protein*

For centuries rice has been the dietary staple of the East, where it provided a basis for good nutrition. It is low in fat, provides protein and most of the B vitamins, but not vitamins A, C, or $B_{12}$. It was traditionally eaten as brown rice, which contains all the nutrients in the germ and outer layers of the grain, but with the arrival of modern milling techniques and the production of white rice, most of the B vitamins (especially thiamin) were lost. Parboiling the rice before milling pushes some of the vitamins back into the grain and reduces the thiamin loss to about 40 percent instead of 80 percent.

Plain boiled brown rice is a universal folk remedy for diarrhea— as is the water in which it is boiled. And boiled rice mixed with puréed apples is recommended by some European doctors as an aid to reducing blood pressure.

The two main types of rice are long-grain and short-grain. Long rice grains are about five times as long as they are wide, while short grains are much more rounded.

American long-grain rice can be used for most dishes and is best cooked by the hot-water method (*see opposite*). Brown rice will take about 30 minutes, while white rice takes 15–20 minutes.

Arborio rice is the Italian variety used to make risotto. Its short grains clump together as they cook and tend to break down more, resulting in a smooth, creamy texture with a distinctive nutty flavor. There is no quick way to make good risotto—you need to stand by the pot, adding liquid gradually and stirring constantly. It's worth the effort.

Basmati is the classic long-grain rice of Indian cooking. It is slightly aromatic with a definite flavor of its own, and the grains separate well when cooked, making them ideal for pilafs and salads. Best cooked by the absorption method, basmati rice takes 15–20 minutes. ▶

**152**

WHITE LONG-GRAIN RICE

BASMATI RICE

PUDDING RICE

**rice continued**

Easy-cook rice has been pre-processed to shorten the cooking time and is designed to cook by the absorption method.

Japanese short-grain rice is the shiny, glutinous rice served in every Japanese restaurant at the end of the meal, or used to prepare the vinegar rice that goes so well with sushi.

Pudding rice is another short-grain variety, which becomes very soft during cooking. White rice takes 20 minutes, brown about 40 minutes. The traditional oven-baked rice pudding takes around an hour and a half.

Thai rice is delicately flavored with jasmine and goes well with European as well as Thai dishes. It is another short-grain rice and is best cooked by the absorption method.

- ✚ *Suitable for those with celiac disease, since it is gluten-free.*
- ✚ *Useful for diarrhea.*
- ✚ *Best cooked until slightly al dente, then eaten hot or cold.*

### COOKING RICE

**The hot-water method:** Add rice to a large saucepan of boiling, lightly salted water. Plenty of water, combined with a large pan, allows the rice grains to move about freely and not stick together. Simmer until the rice is cooked. Pour into a sieve and rinse with boiling water.

**The absorption method:** This method uses a specific amount of water, which is completely absorbed by the time the rice is cooked. Put one measure of rice and two and a half measures of cold water in a saucepan with a pinch of salt. Bring to a boil, stir briskly, cover, and allow to simmer for 15 minutes. Let stand for an additional 15 minutes, fluffing the rice with a fork before serving.

## WILD RICE

**⑤ ⑨**

*Energy per standard portion 248 calories*
*Rich in protein, B vitamins, and minerals*

This is not rice at all, but the seeds of an aquatic freshwater grass, which is native to the Great Lakes region of North America and can be found in shallow lakes and rivers of northeastern United States and eastern Canada. For over a thousand years wild rice was harvested by Native Americans, who bent the willowy grass across their canoes, then tapped it gently so that the grain fell out, leaving the plants unharmed to allow the next lot of seeds to ripen.

Wild rice contains significant quantities of essential minerals including zinc. The long, black grains have a nutty flavor and are more chewy than ordinary rice. Wild rice is expensive, but for a treat serve it mixed with brown rice. Since it needs longer cooking, give it 10 minutes in boiling water before you add the brown rice, then cook as normal.

- ✚ *Good for depression and irritability.*
- ✚ *Beneficial for menstrual problems.*
- ✚ *Best used in salads, mixed with basmati rice, or combined with brown rice.*

### SUPER FOOD

● Wild rice is an incredible nutritional storehouse, containing more protein than even oats or brown rice. Its B-vitamin content exceeds that of most other cereals and it is also rich in the nutritionally valuable linolenic acids.

# DAIRY FOODS
# AND EGGS

*Dairy foods*

*Eggs*

# DAIRY FOODS AND EGGS

**M**ilk, dairy products, and eggs are all popular and easy-to-use foods that are excellent suppliers of the nutrients we need each day. Milk and its products are some of the highest suppliers of calcium, are

CHICKEN EGGS

rich in protein, riboflavin (vitamin $B_2$), vitamin $B_{12}$, and vitamin A (retinol—with slightly smaller amounts of this in low-fat products). Eggs are an inexpensive form of very high-quality protein and are good sources of vitamin A, $B_{12}$, and zinc.

It is worth remembering this when we hear in the press of yet another scare concerning these foods. These concerns range from the methods of production and processing to fat content and some links with food intolerances. But the variety of dairy products available, the versatility of eggs, and stricter controls on production should encourage people to continue to include these foods in their diet.

Many people avoid dairy products and eggs because of their fat content—the saturated fat in milk and milk products, and the cholesterol in eggs; but careful thought should be given to your overall diet before doing so. Bear in mind the importance of a good supply of calcium throughout life, in order to help prevent osteoporosis, and the fact that calcium is most easily obtained from milk and dairy products. If these have to be left out of the diet, then other sources of calcium must be taken instead. And the cholesterol in eggs contributes very little to blood cholesterol, which the body actually manufactures from saturated fats provided by other foods.

For young children, particularly those with small appetites, full-fat milk is a good supplier of energy, along with essential nutrients. For this reason low-fat milk and milk products should not be part of a child's diet before the age of five.

Dairy products and eggs are not consumed universally, and several population groups avoid or restrict some, or all, of these foods for religious or philosophical reasons, or because of a known food intolerance. In some other communities, however, eggs, milk, and dairy products (often made from sheep, goat, or buffalo milk) are valuable

YOGURT WITH FRUIT

sources of protein, vitamin D, and calcium, for people in whose diets these nutrients might otherwise be marginal.

FRESH MILK

## MILK AND CREAM

**6** **9**

WHOLE MILK
*Energy per standard portion 386 calories*

LOW-FAT MILK
*Energy per standard portion 269 calories*

SKIM MILK
*Energy per standard portion 193 calories*
*Rich in protein, calcium, zinc, and riboflavin*

Nutritionally, milk is a valuable source of essential nutrients. It is a cheap and easily consumed, rich source of calcium, protein, zinc, and riboflavin ($B_2$). For the elderly, who may not be eating well, the growing young, for pregnant women, or for active people who rush around all day and burn up nutrients, milk has a vital part to play—3 cups/600ml provides just over half the calcium and vitamin $B_2$ needed by pregnant or breastfeeding women, and more than that needed by everyone else. It also contains more than a day's dose of vitamin $B_{12}$. Roughly one-third of everyone's protein requirements can also be met by the same amount of milk, along with 15 percent of your total energy needs.

Unfortunately there are drawbacks to this apparent wonder-food. Naturopaths have long believed that cow's milk may be a trigger of infantile eczema and catarrh, excessive mucus and chestiness in both children and adults. Studies at the British College of Naturopathy and Osteopathy in Hampstead have shown that breast-feeding mothers consuming a large amount of cow's milk tend to have babies who are more prone to infections such as eczema and chronic catarrh—and who also experience more colic.

Adults are not immune to milk-related problems either, and there are populations throughout the world, especially in India, Japan, and China, where there is frequently an inability to digest cow's milk. This is caused by the lack of a normal digestive enzyme, lactase, which is essential for the breakdown and digestion of the milk sugar, lactose.

But before depriving anyone, especially children or women, of all dairy products seek professional advice to make sure that calcium deficiency does not ensue. ▶

**milk and cream continued**

One of the drawbacks of milk is its high fat content, so it is always better to choose low-fat or skim varieties, even though these contain fewer vitamins A, D, and E than the full-fat product. But for this reason, as well as for the substantial reduction that skim milk shows in calorie content, these fat-reduced milks should not be given to the under-fives.

However, it is not even certain that you will get the full range of nutrients from your milk. Pasteurization loses 25 percent of the vitamin C, and the remaining proportion decreases even further by the time you get your milk home from the store.

Riboflavin (vitamin B₂) is extremely sensitive to ultraviolet light, so if your milk stands for two hours on the doorstep in the sun you lose half of it. Fluorescent lighting also destroys riboflavin, so further losses occur in the stores where the milk is stored in bottles, although this does not seem to happen to cartoned milk. When the riboflavin is broken down, the residual chemicals destroy most of the vitamin C that is left. When all the vitamin C has gone, boiling your milk also puts paid to the folic acid that it contains.

For those whose allergies are triggered by cow's milk, goat's milk is often an acceptable alternative. But take care with babies, because goat's milk contains substantially less folic acid, which is reduced even further by boiling the milk and can result in babies becoming anemic. But any milk is only as good as the food fed to the cows or goats, so whenever possible buy organic milk.

Cream may be delicious, but it is full of calories, most of which come from fat. As an occasional treat it is fine, and it is worth remembering that whipped cream is mostly air and actually contains far less fat than heavy cream. Use it sparingly and enjoy it with relish.

- ✚ *Good for growth, strong bones, and for convalescence.*
- ✚ *Best drunk straight from the refrigerator or used in recipes.*
- ➖ *People with rheumatoid arthritis, eczema, catarrh, sinus problems, and sometimes asthma often find their symptoms aggravated by cow's milk.*

NATURAL YOGURT

## YOGURT

❶ ❷ ❻ ❽ ⑨

LOW-FAT PLAIN YOGURT
*Energy per standard portion 84 calories*

ORGANIC YOGURT
*Energy per standard portion 84 calories*
*Rich in calcium and probiotics*

Yogurt in some form or other has been made since time immemorial. It is an excellent source of calcium, with one 5oz/150g carton providing 210mg—well over a quarter of the minimum daily requirement; for weight-conscious people, low-fat varieties contain even more calcium, at 285mg per carton. Yogurt also contains small traces of vitamin D, which is essential for the absorption of calcium.

Many health problems start in the gut, when the balance between the good bacteria and the bad ones swings in the wrong direction. Most commercial yogurts are made from the starting point of pasteurized milk, which is inoculated with cultures of highly beneficial bacteria like *Lactobacillus acidophilus* or *bulgaricus*, *Bifidobacteria* or *Streptococcus thermophilus*. But many yogurt products, especially those with long sell-by dates, are pasteurized after manufacture, so they contain none of the live and beneficial organisms that give yogurt its unique properties. They comprise a host of chemicals, stabilizers, emulsifiers, artificial flavorings, colorings, preservatives, and large amounts of sugar or artificial sweetener (although even some of the much healthier live yogurts contain a selection of these).

Live, or "bio" yogurts contain the health-giving bacteria that help to restore the balance in the gut. These cultures act in several ways. They synthesize some of the B vitamins, biotin, folic acid, and $B_{12}$; increase the uptake of calcium and magnesium; and regulate bowel function. Their presence in the intestines prevents the development of pathogenic bacteria. Even people who cannot digest milk can normally cope with yogurt, so if you are prescribed a course of antibiotics, do eat a carton of yogurt each day. Antibiotics kill all bugs—good and bad—but yogurt replaces the bacteria your body needs and so helps to prevent the diarrhea caused by sterilizing the gut. ▶

*FRUIT YOGURT*

*YOGHURT WITH FRUIT*

**yogurt continued**

Many women, having suffered years of distress as a result of chronic thrush and cystitis, can testify to the benefits of eating live yogurt on a daily basis. It not only helps to relieve the symptoms of thrush and cystitis, but continuing use also acts as a serious preventative.

And there is a slowly emerging but growing body of serious scientific evidence that suggests another remarkable protective role for the amazing little yogurt bugs. Veterinary scientists have found that these "probiotics" can actually produce enzymes that are absorbed directly through the gut wall, and enhance the activity of the body's immune defense mechanisms. And recent Japanese research suggests that all of these probiotic bugs may be protective against stomach cancer.

✚ *Good for diarrhea (when it is caused by antibiotics), the prevention and treatment of osteoporosis, most general digestive problems, the immune system, thrush, and cystitis.*

✚ *Best eaten regularly as low-fat yogurt (but not for the under-fives), unpasteurized, with unsweetened, puréed fruit added if required.*

### FAST FOOD FACTS

● An effective facial scrub can be made with live yogurt by adding two teaspoons of coarse sea salt to a carton. Stir well, then massage thoroughly into the face. Leave for 15 minutes, then wash off with plenty of cold water.

● For thrush and cystitis, apply small amounts of natural live yogurt to the inflamed areas each night. A couple of teaspoonfuls can even be placed inside the vagina if necessary, which is most easily done using a tampon with its inserter.

CHEDDAR

## CHEESE

**1** **3** **5** **6** **9**

BRIE
*Energy per standard portion 128 calories*

CHEDDAR
*Energy per standard portion 165 calories*

COTTAGE CHEESE
*Energy per standard portion 87 calories*
*Rich in protein, calcium, and vitamin B$_{12}$*

The great combination of excellent cheese, wonderful bread, and a glass of good red wine takes a great deal of beating as food for the mind, body, and spirit. Unfortunately there are some drawbacks, in that most cheeses have a high content of saturated fat, the type that is known to cause cholesterol deposits in the arteries and heart disease. But to me it's very sad that the ever-increasing amount of fat in the Western processed diet has led to an obsession about dairy foods among the health-conscious. As part of a healthy balanced diet, cheese has enormously important contributions to make, so allow yourself to savor the wonders of good cheese.

Making cheese must be one of the most ancient of all food-preparing techniques. In 3000 B.C. the Sumerians made 20 different varieties and it is likely that the earliest shepherds and goatherds were producing soft cheeses from their flocks when these animals were first domesticated around 10,000 B.C. It was another 3,000 years before people domesticated cattle and started to make cheese from cow's milk.

Both the ancient Greeks and Romans developed sophisticated cheeses, but much of the cheesemaker's art was lost during the Dark Ages and survived only among isolated mountain dwellers, in the abbeys and monasteries. Today, happily, there is a huge resurgence of interest in farm-made regional cheeses, and small producers are making wonderful-quality cheeses from cow's, sheep's, and goat's milk, although Britain does not yet have the strict *Appellation d'Origine Contrôlée* applied to the 300 or so French cheeses. But the average Briton consumes a total of only 18lb/8.1kg of cheese per year, whereas in Australia the average is 20¼lb/9.2kg, in ▶

GOAT'S CHEESE

BRIE

**cheese continued**

Canada 33¾lb/15.3kg, in Holland 32½lb/14.8kg, and in France—where they have far less heart disease than in Britain—it is 49lb/22.3kg.

I grow increasingly concerned that many people, especially young women, interpret a low-fat diet as being a no-fat diet and exclude most dairy products from their regular food intake, often in the pursuit of thinness. But as a source of calcium (for building strong bones), of essential protein, vitamin D (to help absorb the calcium), a selection of B vitamins (for the central nervous system), vitamin A (as a cancer-protector and for healthy skin), and a spread of essential minerals, a little good cheese is hard to beat.

There are variations in the nutritional value of cheeses, but it is worth knowing that 3½oz/100g of Cheddar cheese supplies more than a day's dose of calcium, half the required protein, nearly half the zinc, half the vitamin A, one-fifth of the selenium, quarter of the iodine, three-quarters of the vitamin $B_{12}$, and one-fifth of the folate that a woman needs each day.

In general, the harder the cheese, the higher the fat content—with the obvious exception of cream cheese, which is the fattiest of all. Stilton, Cheddar, blue cheese, and Parmesan are all high in fat, but Camembert, Brie, Edam, and Feta contain considerably less. There are now many "low-fat" cheeses made from skim milk, which contain around ½oz/15g of total fat per 3½oz/100g. Cottage cheese contains only 4g per 100g and curd cheese around 11g. Many processed cheeses—they hardly deserve the name anyway—are high in fat, though they are good sources of calcium and protein. ▶

---

**SUPER FOOD**

● Cheese is a very useful source of zinc, which is vital for normal male sexual function; though it is not present in enormous quantities, the zinc is in an easily absorbed bio-available form—3½oz/100g of most cheese provides over a quarter of a man's daily zinc needs.

STILTON

MOZZARELLA

**cheese continued**

➕ Useful for building strong bones, and for both the prevention and treatment of osteoporosis.

➕ A good source of protein, especially for vegetarians.

➕ Good for preconception, pregnancy, and breastfeeding (but not unpasteurized cheeses during pregnancy).

➕ Beneficial for male sexual function.

➕ Best eaten fresh, with good wholewheat bread or with virtually salt-free matzos.

➕ Combines well with most fresh fruit.

➕ Can be eaten cooked either in sauces or as toppings.

➖ Cheeses made from unpasteurized milk may be contaminated with bacteria, particularly Salmonella and Listeria, and anyone with a compromised immune system, pregnant women, the chronically ill, and elderly should avoid them.

➖ Cheeses contain a chemical called tyramine, which can trigger migraine attacks; soft goat's and sheep's cheeses, cottage and cream cheese are usually okay.

➖ Anyone taking monoamine oxidase inhibitors (MAOIs) should avoid cheese, especially very mature hard cheese, since it can cause dramatic increases in blood pressure.

## GOAT'S AND SHEEP'S CHEESE

● Cheese can be made from any milk, but goat's and sheep's milk are the oldest sources for the cheesemaker. Most goat's cheese is eaten very young and soft and has a characteristic taste. As it matures it becomes slightly firmer, developing a stronger flavor with a definite tang.

● Sheep's milk makes delicious and usually mild cheese, but it matures to a much firmer texture. The Spanish Manchega is an exceptional variety—hard with a full, but still mild flavor. French Roquefort, Italian Pecorino, and Greek Feta are strongly flavored sheep's cheeses. Both sheep's and goat's cheeses are lower in fat and lactose. People who cannot tolerate cow's milk cheeses often find them a suitable alternative.

CHICKEN EGGS

DUCK EGGS

# EGGS

**❶ ❹ ❺ ❻ ❾**

CHICKEN EGGS
*Energy per standard portion 90 calories*

DUCK EGGS
*Energy per standard portion 122 calories*

QUAIL EGGS
*Energy per standard portion 75 calories*
*Rich in protein and vitamin B$_{12}$*

How sad it is that the obsession with cholesterol, especially in the United States, has resulted in the humble egg being branded as the villain in the story of heart disease. The confusion arises because of a lack of understanding of the difference between dietary cholesterol and blood cholesterol. There is no doubt that raised levels of blood cholesterol—the cholesterol that the body manufactures from a high intake of saturated animal fat—do increase the risk of coronary heart disease. But the cholesterol in food such as eggs and shellfish (see p. 134) does not add to the circulating blood cholesterol and should not be a concern, except for people who are suffering from high cholesterol levels or those with the hereditary disease that causes them to manufacture far too much cholesterol.

While US and British experts advise eating no more than three or four eggs per week, the World Health Organization advocates a total of 10 (including those used in cooking). Eggs are an amazing source of protein, although it is not the quantity of protein in a food but its quality that is important. Nutritionists use the term NPU—Net Protein Utilization—to measure the biological availability of different protein sources. For example, lentils have an NPU of 30, soybeans of 63, cheese of 70—but eggs are rated at 94, and just two boiled eggs provide more than a quarter of a day's protein for women and over one-fifth for men. Eggs are also a rich source of zinc, vitamins A, D, E, and B, and especially B$_{12}$. This vitamin is often lacking in vegetarian diets, but two eggs, especially if they are free-range, provide more than a day's need of this essential nutrient.

One of the most important substances in egg yolk is lecithin, which is vital as part of many of ▶

QUAIL EGGS

**eggs continued**

the body's metabolic processes, including the dispersal of dangerous fat deposits and cholesterol. Lecithin prevents the development of heart disease and the formation of gallstones and encourages the speedy conversion of body fats into energy. It also makes eggs an important brain food, which contributes not only to memory and concentration, but also to a balanced mental and emotional status.

Whether you choose hen, duck, quail, gull, or goose eggs, they are all nutritionally similar. The one exception is factory-farmed battery hens, whose eggs contain less vitamin B$_{12}$ and all the extras in the artificial feed on which these poor creatures live. There is also a much higher risk of *Salmonella* infection from intensively reared hens so, unless you are quite certain that yours are genuinely free-range, eggs should be eaten thoroughly cooked.

✚ *Good for rheumatoid arthritis and osteoarthritis.*
✚ *Useful for cancer and heart protection, and for anemia.*
✚ *Beneficial for male sexual function.*
✚ *Best eaten boiled or poached to avoid added fat.*

➖ *Eggs are quite a common cause of allergy and introducing eggs too early in a baby's diet may increase the risk; in some children asthma attacks can also be triggered by eggs.*
➖ *Beware Salmonella: pregnant women, infants and children, the elderly, and anyone with a compromised immune system should take great care only to eat eggs that have been boiled, poached, or fried until the yolks are hard.*

## FAST FOOD FACTS

● Eggs are an excellent and cheap natural beauty product. For dry hair, whisk one egg together with a cup of beer and apply after shampooing for beautifully conditioned, glossy hair.
● For oily skin, whisk the white of one egg together with the juice of half a lemon and apply to the face for five minutes (avoiding the area around the eyes) for a wonderfully astringent face mask.

# HERBS, SPICES, VINEGARS, AND FATS

*Herbs*

*Spices*

*Vinegars*

*Fats and oils*

# HERBS, SPICES, VINEGARS, AND FATS

The history of herbs, spices, and condiments is as old as the history of civilization—practically all diets include seasonings, flavorings, and sauces made from herbs, spices, and other edible substances, such as vinegar, which have aromatic or pungent flavours, aromas, and colors. The consumption of herbs, spices, and condiments varies greatly in different parts of the world, inversely in proportion to the consumption of salt. But making more imaginative use of such flavorings in food preparation could go a long way to reducing both salt and fat in our diet.

Many traditional cuisines are typified by their use of herbs, spices, and condiments, used either singly or in combination, mixed into food while cooking or at the table. In addition to making ordinary foods delicious, herbs, spices, and vinegars are valued for their functions as preservatives, in medicines and tonics. In some societies they are mixed with food in various combinations and quantities in order to prevent or treat common diseases, and many popular pharmaceuticals are derived from herbs and other plants.

BAY LEAF

CAYENNE

*Though various herbs contain carotenoids and vitamin C, because they make up only a small part by volume and weight they do not make a significant contribution to the diet in terms of nutrients. However, herbs, spices, and vinegars all contain a number of bioactive compounds, which— although their activity may be poorly understood—are now being recognized and included in scientific studies, including cancer research.*

*Fat is the most energy-dense constituent of our diet. The more industrialized and urbanized a society becomes, the greater the amount of energy contributed by fats and oils. Fats may be classified by their chemical composition as containing varying proportions of saturated, polyunsaturated, and mono-unsaturated fatty acids. They may also be classified as being of either plant or animal origin. Some fats perform a vital role in cell-membrane synthesis, particularly of nerve tissue. But it is the overconsumption of fats and oils (particularly of saturated fatty acids) in some industrialized societies that is negatively linked with obesity, coronary heart disease, and some cancers.*

BUTTER

## BALM

**2 5**

*Rich in volatile oils*

Otherwise known as lemon balm, this herb is equally helpful for calming nervous tension or the anxious indigestion that so often accompanies it; it is also very beneficial in the treatment of mild to moderate depression. It is useful for children's problems too—in Spain it is considered a nursery cure-all.

Use the leaves to make a soothing tea and enjoy the delicate aroma of citronella and the other flavonoids in the plant. It is the volatile oils that give lemon balm its wonderful smell.

➕ *Good for stressful situations, depression, and nervous indigestion.*
➕ *Best added to salads or drunk as herbal tea.*

### FAST FOOD FACTS

● A traditional treatment for the painful swellings of gout is a compress soaked in warm lemon-balm tea and applied to the inflamed area.
● You can also use lemon-balm leaf in order to soothe insect bites and stings.

## ANGELICA

**2 4 6 7 9**

*Rich in tannins and volatile oils*

This can be taken either as an infused tea, which makes an excellent remedy for indigestion, or as a tincture—a small teaspoonful three times a day for mild chest infections. Angelica contains volatile oils, a little vitamin A and B, and is rich in tannins. Herbalists often use the dried root in the treatment of liver disorders, arthritis, and as a gentle stimulant. American angelica (*Angelica atropurpurea*) is an effective remedy for wind and heartburn. Pungent Chinese angelica (*Dang gui*) brings great relief from menstrual discomfort and is used by the Chinese to treat anemia.

➕ *Good for digestive problems, chest infections, arthritis, and anemia.*
➕ *Best eaten in candied form, as a decoration for cakes, or drunk as tea.*
➖ *Diabetics should avoid angelica; it can push the blood-sugar level up.*

### FAST FOOD FACT

● Sprinkle a few angelica leaves into your bath to ease the pain of aching joints.

## BAY

❷

*Rich in volatile oils*

The distinctive flavor of bay leaves is an intrinsic part of the classic French *bouquet garni,* and they are prized as much for their antiseptic properties as for their assistance in digestion, helping to ward off gas and cramps. Bay contains the volatile oils geraniol, cimeol, and eugenol. When used in recipes its stimulation of the digestive juices improves the absorption of nutrients from the food.

Bay leaves are a most beneficial addition to the diets of people recovering from serious illness, and especially anorexia nervosa.

➕ *Valuable for the digestion and for convalescents.*
➕ *Best added to soups and stews or used in a* bouquet garni.
➖ *Essential oil of bay can cause allergic reactions and should only be used in very dilute mixtures. Test a small patch of skin before using. On no account take it internally.*

### FAST FOOD FACT

● Add a decoction of bay leaves to a hot bath in order to relieve aches and pains.

## MINT

❷ ❺

*Rich in essential oils*

This herb contains the essential oils menthol, menthone, menthyl acetate, and flavonoids. Soothing to the stomach, mint is helpful in irritable bowel syndrome, spasm of the muscles of the intestine and colon. Peppermint tea made from fresh leaves and taken after meals is popular throughout the Middle East as an aid to good digestion. Mint tea is also used to relieve headaches, especially when caused by stress.

➕ *Good for the digestion and to relieve stress.*
➕ *Best eaten as a sauce with lamb, added to desserts to bring out their flavor, or drunk as tea.*
➖ *Some people may be allergic to contact with peppermint oil, so always do a small patch test first. Do not use on babies.*

### FAST FOOD FACT

● Peppermint oil, when diluted five drops to 1fl oz/25ml of grapeseed oil, makes a good rub for tired, aching muscles or, massaged into the temples, relieves headaches.

## CAMOMILE

② ③ ⑤ ⑦ ⑨

*Rich in volatile oils*

Insomnia, nervous indigestion, and the jitters all respond well to this magically calming herb, which contains volatile oils, flavonoids, tannins, and cumarins. It makes one of the most pleasant of all herbal teas, and will also help with bloating, stomachache, and even, suitably diluted, with baby colic. It also has a good anti-inflammatory action, which helps with joint problems and period pains. As a remedy for sleepless children, high temperatures, and general irritability, it is hard to better and can even reduce the severity of hay fever symptoms.

➕ *Beneficial for the nerves, the digestion, and skin problems.*
➕ *Best drunk as tea.*

### FAST FOOD FACTS

● Three camomile teabags in a warm bath relieve the terrible itching of eczema.
● A strong infusion of camomile can be used as a mouthwash in order to soothe inflammations of the mouth.
● As an inhalation, camomile can help relieve nasal catarrh.

## BORAGE

③ ⑥ ⑦ ⑧ ⑨

*Rich in gamma linoleic acid*

Borage helps reduce high temperatures, stimulates the kidneys, and aids chronic chest problems. It contains a number of alkaloids as well as tannins and mucilage, but most interestingly large amounts of gamma linoleic acid (GLA). Their presence makes borage a good remedy for PMS, rheumatoid arthritis, and eczema. Borage tea is an aid to more restful sleep.

➕ *Useful for chest and skin problems, PMS, and high temperatures.*
➕ *Best used as an edible garnish for chilled soups, in salads, or the mixed drink Pimms.*
➖ *The alkaloids can be toxic and the fresh leaves can cause contact dermatitis, so wear gloves when picking it.*

### FAST FOOD FACT

● For dry, scaly skin, place your head under a towel and over a bowl with 10 cups/2l of boiling water and a couple of handfuls of borage leaves. Steam your face for 8–10 minutes, then rinse with cool water.

## CHIVES
### ❷
*Rich in sulfur compounds*

This herb shares many of the wonderful healing properties of garlic and onions, which belong to the same *Allium* family of plants. When used as a seasoning in cooking, chives should not be added until the last minute or their uniquely delicate flavor is lost. They have an antiseptic action, and both their smell and taste improve the appetite and encourage the flow of digestive juices.

## BASIL
### ❷ ❸
*Rich in volatile oils*

Basil contains volatile oils, especially linalol, limonene, and estragole. It is good for flatulence, helps digestion, and its antiseptic properties are said to benefit acne. It is also a mild sedative and makes an excellent evening snack to help those suffering from insomnia: tear up three or four leaves into small pieces and add them to a sandwich of lettuce and tomato for a natural tranquilizing effect.

## CORIANDER
### ❷ ❺ ❽
*Rich in volatile oils*

Of all the spices to be grown in the United States, coriander was among the first. Both the seeds and leaves are used, though they have very different flavors. This strongly aromatic plant contains linalol, pinene, terpinine, and flavoncids. It is one of the most popular of all the food plants of India, the fresh leaves being sprinkled over curries. Ayurvedic physicians use coriander as a diuretic, as a digestive aid, and to enhance male potency.

- ✚ *Beneficial for the digestion, male potency, and stress.*
- ✚ *Best used in curries, sauces, and in salads.*

### FAST FOOD FACTS

● Tea made from one heaped teaspoon of chopped coriander leaves in a cup of boiling water helps with wind, irritable bowel syndrome, and stress.
● And one teaspoon of crushed and roasted seeds in a glass of warm water makes a good gargle for oral thrush.

**173**

## DILL

❷

*Rich in volatile oils*

Dill contains the volatile oils carvone, limonene, and phellandrine, as well as cumarins and xanthones. It is extremely effective in the relief of gripe, flatulence, and stomach pain. Babies can be given dill in the form of gripe water.

## FENNEL

❷ ❽

*Rich in volatile oils*

Fennel contains volatile oils and some flavonoids. It makes an exceptional aid for flatulence, stimulates the liver, and improves the digestion. And an infusion of the seeds is helpful for kidney stones and cystitis. In the past the leaves, roots, and seeds were all eaten to improve fitness and help in weight control.

➖ *Excessive amounts of fennel seeds can be toxic, so do not exceed the recommended dose.*

## MARJORAM AND OREGANO

❺ ❼

*Rich in essential oils*

*Origanum vulgare*, known as oregano throughout the Mediterranean and in the United States, is the original wild oregano. In Britain the same plant is known as wild marjoram. It was taken to America by the early settlers, where its name was changed in the 1940s.

Oregano contains highly active essential oil with a number of components, including thymol, carvacrol, and origanene, and it is these constituents that make it such an important medicinal plant. It has a powerful antiseptic action and is very effective in the treatment of all respiratory problems, coughs, bronchitis, and even asthma. A cup of oregano tea is an instant answer to anxiety and nervousness. With a little honey, it is also a perfect relaxing bedtime drink for insomniacs. And chewing a leaf or two can help alleviate toothache.

➕ *Valuable for the nerves and for respiratory problems.*

➕ *Best used in stuffings, on pizzas, or drunk as tea.*

## PARSLEY
**6 8 9**

*Rich in essential oils, vitamins A and C*

Parsley contains the essential oils apiole, myristicin, and limonene, as well as cumarins and flavonoids. It is also rich in vitamins A and C, iron, calcium, and potassium. Traditionally used as a diuretic and anti-inflammatory, it is also a strong antioxidant. By aiding the elimination of uric acid it is useful in treating rheumatism and gout. I recommend parsley, celery, carrot, and apple juice to patients with fluid retention just before the onset of menstruation.

Parsley tea makes a gentle, natural diuretic; drink a glass every three hours. The seeds are also diuretic, and can be used just like celery seeds.

✚ *A useful diuretic and anti-inflammatory.*
✚ *Best used in salads or on vegetables, or drunk as tea.*
➖ *Large doses of parsley seeds can be toxic; avoid them if you have kidney disease or are pregnant.*

### FAST FOOD FACT

● Chew a few leaves of parsley to freshen the breath after onions, garlic, or too much alcohol.

## ROSEMARY
**2 4 5**

*Rich in volatile oils*

Rosemary is both a tonic and stimulant of the brain's cortex, easing general debility, improving memory loss by enhancing the cellular uptake of oxygen, and reducing nervous tension. It contains the volatile oils borneol, camphor, limonene, flavonoids, and rosemaricene. Rosemary is also anti-inflammatory, stimulates the gall bladder and increases the flow of bile, so aiding fat digestion. And rosemary tea is an excellent natural remedy for headaches.

Rosemary also aids good circulation and strengthens weak blood vessels. It is used in many herbal shampoos because of its refreshing, tonic quality, and an infusion of rosemary with borax can be used as a rinse to treat dandruff.

✚ *Benefits the nervous system, digestion, and circulation.*
✚ *Best used with lamb and chicken.*

### FAST FOOD FACT

● Hang a bunch of fresh sprigs under running water to make your bath invigorating.

## SAGE

② ④ ⑦ ⑨

*Rich in volatile oils*

Sage stimulates the bile and improves the digestion of fats. It contains volatile oils, thujone, bitters, flavonoids, and phenolic acids and is a cleansing antiseptic and anti-inflammatory herb. Herbalists use it to help with menstrual problems, to reduce excessive sweating, and for chest infections. The thujone is a phytoestrogen, so consumption of sage on a regular basis helps women control menopausal hot flushes.

Red sage, a Chinese relative known as *Dan shen*, contains tanshirones, which improve the efficiency of the heart by stimulating coronary circulation. It is also powerfully antiseptic and makes a very effective gargle for sore throats. Sage tea can also be used as an effective mouthwash for gum infections and mouth ulcers.

➕ *Good for menstrual problems, the digestion, and chest infections.*
➕ *Best used in stuffings with rich meats like pork and venison, in sausages, or drunk as tea.*
➖ *Sage can interfere with the flow of breast milk, so don't overuse this herb when breastfeeding.*

## THYME

② ⑦

*Rich in essential oils*

This herb is used as a tea and very widely used in cooking. It contains the essential oils thymol (still widely used as a base for many antiseptics and mouthwashes) and carvacrol, as well as flavonoids. It helps in the breakdown of fats, and thymol and carvol have a specific effect on the smooth muscle of the trachea, which explains the expectorant benefits of thyme. Thyme oil is widely used in pharmaceutical products, as well as for flavoring. Tea made from thyme makes a good gargle for sore throats and mouth ulcers.

➕ *Beneficial for sore throats, coughs, and catarrh.*
➕ *Best used in a bouquet garni or added to stews, marinades, and chicken dishes.*
➖ *Essential oil of thyme is toxic—do not take it internally; if you are pregnant do not use the essential oil for massage or in the bath.*

### FAST FOOD FACT

● For rheumatic aches and pains add five drops of thyme oil to a hot bath.

# SPICES
*Prized as flavorings*

L ike herbs, spices have a long history of culinary and medicinal use, and may be used to flavor both savory and sweet dishes. Spices were originally used to disguise putrefaction in the days before canning, dehydration, and freezing, since some spices contain essential oils, which either inhibit the growth of microorganisms or are toxic to them. Other spices were traditionally used to correct a variety of intestinal disorders, because of their antimicrobial activity, and such remedies were handed down from generation to generation. The oils from some spices are also used in perfumes and cosmetics.

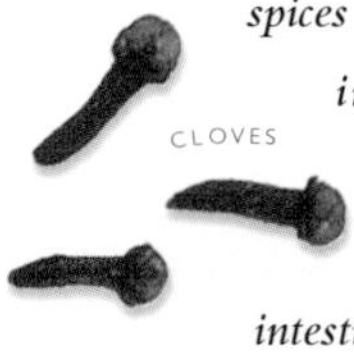

So although spices have little nutritional value and are used only in very small amounts, they should not be dismissed as insignificant. Care should be taken in using them, however, because some spices are toxic internally and externally, as noted in the individual descriptions that follow.

With their exotic scents and intense flavors, spices should form a greater part of our cooking. The best flavor is obtained from freshly ground spices, so they should always be bought in small quantities. They may be purchased already in combination (such as mixed spice, curry powder, or garam masala); but the ideal solution is to mix your own and experiment with this range of aromatic seasonings.

MUSTARD

CLOVES

CINNAMON

## CARDAMOM

❷ ❹ ❼

*Rich in aromatic oils*

Cardamom is helpful for all digestive problems, especially diarrhea, colic, and gas. The pods are used equally in sweet and savory dishes, and in India they form a vital ingredient of many curry dishes. In Ayurvedic medicine, cardamom seeds are regarded as a cardio-tonic and an expectorant. Chewing a few cardamom seeds cleans the mouth and disguises the odor of the breath.

## ANISE

❷ ❼

*Rich in essential oils*

Also called aniseed, its flavor and medicinal value come from the essential oils, anethole and estragol. The seeds are helpful for dry coughs and for breaking up mucus. Tea made from the seeds relieves flatulence, boosts the appetite, and aids digestion.

## CARAWAY

❷ ❼ ❽

*Rich in carvone, limonene, and pinene*

In Central Europe caraway seeds are a well-known aid to digestion. They contain the compounds carvone, limonene, and pinene, which make them effective in coping with wind or flatulence. Add them to potentially windy dishes, such as cabbage or beans, or make an infusion of them to soothe indigestion. They are a gentle diuretic, an expectorant, and are often used in children's cough remedies.

✚ *Valuable for respiratory and digestive problems.*
✚ *Best used sprinkled over rich meat, in soups, and in baking.*

### FAST FOOD FACT

● A mixture of five drops of essential oil to 1fl oz/25ml of grapeseed oil is useful in the treatment of scabies.

## CINNAMON

*Rich in volatile oil*

This spice is a stimulant, a tonic, and an antiseptic. It warms the whole system and helps combat the fatigue and listlessness that so often accompany a bout of flu or other viral infections. Bruise a stick of cinnamon and add it to a hot, sweet toddy at the start of a cold, or whenever you feel low. Its most important constituent is the volatile oil cinnamaldehyde, which has a mild sedative effect, acts as a painkiller, and helps to lower raised blood pressure. Cinnamon is also a digestive aid and helps to control sickness and diarrhea. Ayurvedic practitioners traditionally use it in the treatment of anorexia and as an expectorant.

➕ *Good for coughs, digestive problems, fatigue, and listlessness.*

➕ *Best used in baked and fruit desserts, teas, punches, and some meat and fish dishes.*

### FAST FOOD FACT

● A cinnamon stick boiled in water produces an excellent steam inhalation for blocked sinuses and chesty coughs.

## CAYENNE

*Rich in capsaicin*

This fiery spice has always been popular with herbalists for use in acute illness, where the body becomes chilled and the pulse slows down. The chemical constituent capsaicin accounts for cayenne's amazing ability to stimulate the circulation and help those with chilblains. Capsicidins from the seeds also have quite a strong antibacterial power. Cayenne acts as a digestive stimulant and helps to protect against stomach bugs and food poisoning.

➕ *Useful for circulatory problems and to stimulate the digestion.*

➕ *Best used sparingly in soups, stews, and savory dishes.*

➖ *People with sensitive skins can react to hot peppers, so wear gloves when preparing cayenne.*

### FAST FOOD FACT

● For a warming massage oil, add 2oz/50g of finely chopped chili pepper to 1 cup/250ml grapeseed oil and infuse gently over hot water for at least one hour. Strain into a dark glass bottle; keep cool. Use sparingly.

## CLOVES

*Rich in eugenole*

Cloves are a powerful antiseptic and a warming stimulant to the circulation. Add a bruised clove or two to any herbal tea to give you an extra lift. Its major constituent is the volatile oil eugenole. The Indians, like the Chinese, regarded cloves highly as a breath freshener, and their use in the Indian spice garam masala imparts a distinctive taste to Indian cooking. Ayurvedic practitioners knew about the clove's ability to ease toothache long before clove oil became a popular remedy in the West.

➕ *Valuable as an antiseptic and a stimulant to the circulation.*

➕ *Best used in the Indian spice mixture garam masala, in stewed fruit, marinades, and pickling.*

### FAST FOOD FACTS

● For the treatment of boils, dab two or three drops of essential oil onto the surface of the boil.

● For toothache, either chew a clove or rub a couple of drops of essential oil around the affected tooth and repeat as necessary.

## MUSTARD

*Rich in sinigrin*

Mustard seeds contain sinigrin, which is converted to allyl isothiocyanate, which gives mustard its taste, smell, and inflammatory qualities. Most modern medicinal use is external, though mustard is both diuretic and emetic (induces vomiting). Mustard flour mixed to a paste with water can be spread on cloth and applied to the lower back for lumbago and sciatica, to the chest for bronchitis and pneumonia, and elsewhere for neuralgia. Used as a condiment, mustard stimulates the gastric juices and so aids the digestion.

➕ *Good for chest complaints and relieving aches and pains.*

➕ *Best used as a strong flavoring for sauces and pickles.*

➖ *Mustard may cause blistering on the skin, so test a small area before using mustard poultices.*

### FAST FOOD FACT

● Add two teaspoons of mustard powder to a large bowl of hot water to make an invigorating foot bath for the relief of headaches, colds, and flu.

## HORSERADISH

*Rich in siligrin and sulfur*

This belongs to the same species, Cruciferae, as watercress, and shares many of its tonic and curative powers, including a strong antibiotic action. Its powerful antibacterial and cancer-protective properties come from its siligrin content, which breaks down to form isothiocyanates.

The plant is rich in sulfur and its traditional English use as a condiment with roast meats and oily fish acts as an aid to their digestion. Horseradish is a wonderful remedy for coughs, flu, and sinus problems: put one teaspoon of fresh grated root with some honey in a cup of boiling water.

✛ *Beneficial for colds, for the digestion, and as an antibacterial.*

✛ *Best used as a strong sauce with meat and oily fish.*

➖ *Contact with the skin can cause blistering.*

➖ *Those with thyroid problems should use sparingly; it contains goitrogens.*

### FAST FOOD FACT

● A poultice of grated horse-radish steeped in hot water can be applied to unbroken chilblains.

## JUNIPER

*Rich in aromatic oils*

These tiny berries give gin its unique flavor and they impart a powerful tang when used in cooking. Herbalists use them as a stimulating diuretic for diseases of the urinary tract, particularly cystitis. They can be used for rheumatism or gout, since they promote the excretion of uric acid. Like so many culinary herbs, they are a tonic to the digestive system.

✛ *Good for urinary infections, rheumatism, gout, and the digestion.*

✛ *Best used in marinades for game or stuffings for poultry.*

➖ *Do not take juniper if you suffer from kidney disease or acute urinary infection, or are pregnant.*

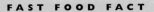

### FAST FOOD FACT

● Essential oil of juniper—five drops to 1fl oz/25ml of grapeseed oil—is helpful when massaged over areas of cellulite, since it speeds up the elimination of waste products stored under the skin. Do not use juniper oil externally if you are pregnant.

## NUTMEG AND MACE

❷ ❸

*Rich in myristicin*

These spices both come from the same plant, the evergreen tree *Myristica fragrans*. The flavor and smell of nutmeg and mace are much the same, although mace tastes slightly more bitter. The major component of nutmeg in terms of its effects on the body is myristicin, which has a profound effect on the brain and is chemically similar to mescalen (from the famous peyote cactus in Mexico). Nutmeg stimulates the appetite and is a valuable digestive remedy for food poisoning, diarrhea, and nausea. In Indian Ayurvedic medicine it is regarded as extremely important for a glowing skin. It is also added to traditional remedies for insomnia, coughs, and nausea.

➕ *Beneficial for the digestive system and for the skin.*

➕ *Best used in milk and cheese dishes.*

➖ *Both spices are highly toxic in large quantities, so use sparingly in food.*

### FAST FOOD FACT

● For severe food poisoning, add a little nutmeg to peppermint tea and drink every four hours.

## GINGER

❶ ❾

*Rich in zingiberene, gingerols, and shogaols (dried ginger)*

Widely used in all Asian cooking, ginger is a common ingredient in both sweet and savory dishes. It is useful for the relief of coughs and colds, is generally a warming plant, and is extremely valuable in the prevention of travel sickness and early-morning sickness during pregnancy. Fresh ginger grated into hot lemon and honey as a bedtime drink can stop a cold in its tracks. Dried ginger is even more pungent than the fresh root.

➕ *Beneficial for the relief of coughs, colds, and nausea.*

➕ *Good added to both sweet and savory dishes.*

### FAST FOOD FACT

● For morning, travel, and post-operative sickness, and as a warming drink, peel and grate $^{1}/_{2}$in/1cm of ginger root into a cup; add boiling water, cover, and stand for ten minutes; strain, add 1 teaspoon of honey and sip slowly.

## SALT

*Harmful in excess*

Salt is a chemical substance called sodium chloride and, although sodium is necessary for the efficient functioning of the body, it is also the sodium that causes problems. When there is too much, the kidneys work harder to get rid of it, the heart pumps more blood through the kidneys, and the blood pressure goes up. Since none of us needs to add salt to our food—there is more than enough there naturally—it makes sense to reduce our salt consumption as much as possible.

Eating too much salt causes high blood pressure, strokes, and heart attacks. Salt also aggravates the fluid retention that occurs around period time and also in heart failure. Too much salt is linked to cancer of the stomach, makes asthma worse, causes loss of calcium from the body, and is a major factor leading to osteoporosis (brittle bone disease). Professor MacGregor of St. George's Hospital, London, believes we should halve our average salt consumption, from 1/4oz/10g to 1/8oz/5g (which is just a teaspoonful) a day. We actually need a mere 1g daily.

But it is not that easy, since most of our salt is added by food manufacturers during processing. It is the most widely used legal substance that puts your health at risk. Some of the worst offenders are takeout meals and processed foods. Look at food labels carefully. The nearer the top of the list of ingredients that salt is, the more salt there is in that particular food. And watch out for monosodium glutamate, saccharin, baking soda, baking powder, sodium nitrate, and many others—all of these substances contain sodium. Food manufacturers often show "mg of sodium per 100g [3½oz]" and this looks deceptively small. Multiply by 2.5 and you will get the amount of salt.

- ⊕ *Necessary for the healthy functioning of the body systems.*
- ⊖ *Best replaced in cooking with savory and aromatic herbs.*
- ⊖ *Excessive salt intake causes high blood pressure, strokes, and heart attacks.*
- ⊖ *Aggravates fluid retention, and is linked to cancer of the stomach, asthma, and osteoporosis.*

# VINEGARS

*Prized for their acetic acid content and preservative properties*

Vinegar is the oldest of all known flavorings and is also an invaluable way of preserving food, since it lasts indefinitely once it has been sealed. Since our earliest beginnings we have practiced the art of vinegar-making: in earliest China and Japan, and in the ancient Greek and Roman civilizations, this age-old craft flourished. The word "vinegar" comes from the Latin words Vinum acer, meaning "sharp wine."

All vinegars start with alcoholic liquid, which is acidified using a group of microorganisms that are called acetobacter, ending up with 4–6 percent acetic acid in the finished product. Although much modern vinegar is produced by high-tech industry, the very best-quality vinegars are still made by the Orléans process, which has not changed in centuries and is extremely slow, taking at least three months before the necessary acidity is reached.

The sharp tangy taste of vinegar is an excellent fat-free dressing for salads, adding extra flavor for those on a low-fat

WHITE WINE VINEGAR

RED WINE VINEGAR

diet who must avoid mayonnaise; all of the true vinegars may also be infused with spices, herbs, or fruit to create a variety of flavors. Chilies, garlic, rosemary, tarragon, bay leaves, and even fruits such as raspberries and strawberries can all be added, and it is fun to experiment with them.

## BALSAMIC VINEGAR

❷

*Energy per standard portion 1 calorie*
*Rich in acetic acid*

Little known outside its home town of Modena in northern Italy until recent years, balsamic vinegar has however long been popular with great chefs and gourmets and highly prized by Italians. It is made from grape must, which should ideally come from the Trebbiano grape. The whole procedure takes a minimum of 12 years, during which the must is aged in wooden barrels, and the very best balsamic vinegars can be up to 50 years old, so it is not surprising that this vinegar is expensive. However, its sweet-and-sour flavor, wonderful aroma, and dark color make it superb for drizzling over delicate salad leaves, a fresh artichoke, or a dish of roasted red bell peppers.

✚ *Valuable as a method of preserving.*
✚ *A useful flavoring.*
✚ *Best used on salads and vegetables.*

### FAST FOOD FACT

● Vinegar is a good antiseptic and, with the addition of garlic, a powerful antifungal for conditions such as athlete's foot.

## CIDER VINEGAR

❷ ❻

*Energy per standard portion 1 calorie*
*Rich in acetic acid*

This is particularly popular in the United States, where the starting alcohol is cider or apple wine. It is not as acidic as malt vinegar but has a distinctive, crisp flavor that is reminiscent of some of the old-fashioned varieties of apple. Cider vinegar is perfect combined with a good olive oil to make light, delicate salad dressings. It is also one of the great traditional home remedies of North America, where it is used for the relief of rheumatism and arthritis: in his best-selling book *Folk Medicine*, Dr. D.C. Jarvis advocates two teaspoons of apple cider vinegar and two of pure honey dissolved in a glass of hot water, to be taken three times a day with meals and at bedtime.

## RICE VINEGAR

❷

*Energy per standard portion 1 calorie*
*Rich in acetic acid*

The traditional vinegar of the Far East, this can be made from rice itself, or from rice wine (sake). It is less acidic than other vinegars and is a delicate accompaniment to Chinese and Japanese food.

## MALT VINEGAR

*Energy per standard portion 1 calorie*
*Rich in acetic acid*

This is the most common variety in Britain and is the vinegar people sprinkle on their fish and chips and use to pickle onions, gherkins, or walnuts. Malt vinegar is made by fermenting malted barley with yeast and then adding the acetobacter cultures, and may be given a darker color by the addition of caramel. Distilled malt vinegar is a clear distillation of ordinary malt vinegar, and is commonly used for pickling and preserving.

➕ *Good for preserving food.*
➕ *Best used in pickling, or over fish and chips.*

WHITE WINE VINEGAR

RED WINE VINEGAR

## SYNTHETIC VINEGAR

*Energy per standard portion 1 calorie*
*Rich in artificial coloring*
*and flavorings*

This is not made by fermentation and is not really vinegar. It is known commercially as NBC (non-brewed condiment) and is usually what is at the local fast-food restaurants. It is artificially colored with caramel, then flavored with sugar, artificial flavorings, and salt.

➖ *Best avoided, particularly by people with allergies or hyperactive children.*

## WINE VINEGAR

*Energy per standard portion 1 calorie*
*Rich in acetic acid*

Wine vinegar starts with low-alcohol wine to which the cultures are added. It is a slow process, which takes place in wooden barrels and results in the end product containing a large number of aromatic compounds, which give good wine vinegar its wonderful flavor. All of the real vinegars, with the exception of balsamic, can be flavored and spiced to suit specific purposes, with chilies, herbs, and even fruits.

# FATS AND OILS

*Prized for their vitamin and
essential fatty acid content*

The whole question of fats is complicated and confusing,
but understanding the different types of fats—saturated,
polyunsaturated, monounsaturated, trans;
cholesterol, high-density lipoprotein,
low-density lipoprotein; omega-3,
omega-6—is a vital step on the road to
nutritional good health. Without some
fats in our diet we cannot absorb the
fat-soluble vitamins A, D, E, and K.

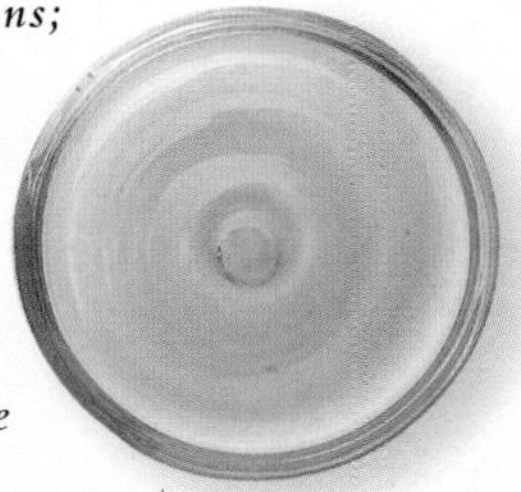

VEGETABLE OIL

Of all the components of our food, fat contains the highest
number of calories by weight and more than twice as many
calories as starchy foods. But a low-fat diet does not mean a
no-fat diet, and those who avoid all fat are just as much at risk
of experiencing serious disease as the overweight, fat-eating
segment of the population.

The first step in reducing fat consumption is to cut down on
all the visible fats—such as butter, cheese, cream, the fat around
your steak or chop or on the outside of a slice of ham. Much
more difficult is to avoid the hidden fats in meat products,
cookies, cakes, and chocolates. The only way is to read
all food labels very carefully. Before you set off for
the supermarket, look at the chart overleaf to
see how little you need to eat of high-fat
foods to provide just 1/4oz/10g of
fat—one-third of your total
recommended consumption
for a day.

BUTTER

## FAT FACTS

| FOOD | AMOUNT CONTAINING $^{1}\!/_{4}$oz/10g of fat |
|------|------|
| Butter | $^{1}\!/_{4}$oz/12g |
| Butter cookie | $1^{1}\!/_{2}$oz/40g |
| Cheddar | 1oz/30g |
| Cheesecake | 1oz/30g |
| Chocolate cookies | $1^{1}\!/_{4}$oz/35g |
| Chocolate Graham crackers | $1^{1}\!/_{2}$oz/40g |
| Cream cheese | $^{3}\!/_{4}$oz/20g |
| French fries (frozen) | 2oz/50g |
| Fried bacon | $^{3}\!/_{4}$oz/20g |
| Fried scampi | 2oz/55g |
| Ground beef | $2^{1}\!/_{2}$oz/60g |
| Heavy cream | $^{3}\!/_{4}$oz/20g |
| Lamb cutlet with fat | 1oz/30g |
| Lard | $^{1}\!/_{4}$oz/10g |
| Light cream | 2oz/50g |
| Margarine | $^{1}\!/_{4}$oz/12g |
| Mayonnaise | $^{1}\!/_{4}$oz/12g |
| Milk chocolate | $1^{1}\!/_{4}$oz/35g |
| Peanut butter | $^{2}\!/_{3}$oz/18g |
| Potato chips | 1oz/30g |
| Quiche | $1^{1}\!/_{4}$oz/35g |
| Roast duck with skin | $^{3}\!/_{4}$oz/25g |
| Sausage | 1oz/30g |
| Savoury meat pie | 2oz/50g |
| Sponge cake | $1^{1}\!/_{2}$oz/40g |
| Stilton cheese | $^{3}\!/_{4}$oz/25g |
| Thousand island dressing | $^{3}\!/_{4}$oz/20g |
| Vegetable oil | $^{1}\!/_{4}$oz/10g |

LARD

SUNFLOWER OIL

OLIVE OIL

## SATURATED FATS
*Harmful in excess*

Saturated fats are nearly all animal fats, butter, lard, the fat on your meat, and the fat in your cheese, cream, and milk. Some vegetables also produce saturated fat, especially coconut and palm. The body is able to manufacture its own saturated fatty acids, so you do not actually need to eat them.

- *Best avoided in direct form.*
- *Linked with heart disease and breast cancer.*

## POLYUNSATURATED FATS
*Rich in fat-soluble vitamins A, D, E, and K*

Polyunsaturated fats are found mainly in vegetable oils like soybean, corn, sunflower, and safflower. They also occur in oily fish and, although containing virtually as many calories as saturated fats, are extremely important and should form a regular part of your diet.

- *Provide essential fatty acids for healthy skin and the development of body cells.*
- *Best eaten as vegetable oils and oily fish.*

## MONOUNSATURATED FATS
*Rich in fat-soluble vitamins A, D, E, and K*

Monounsaturated fats occur mostly in olive oil, canola oil, nuts, and seeds and are important as heart-protectors. The enormous consumption of olive oil in all Mediterranean countries is thought to be one of the factors that results in a much lower level of heart disease in these southern countries than those that occur in northern Europe and North America.

- *Useful as a heart-protector.*
- *Provide essential fatty acids for healthy skin and the development of body cells.*
- *Best eaten as olive or canola oil, in avocados, nuts, and seeds.*

**189**

OILY FISH

MARGARINE

## ESSENTIAL FATTY ACIDS
*Rich in omega-6 and omega-3*

Essential fatty acids are the omega-6 and omega-3 fatty acids, which are vital building blocks of body cells, especially brain and central-nervous-system tissue. They are found in both monounsaturated and polyunsaturated fats. Without them normal development of a baby's brain during pregnancy and in early childhood can be adversely affected.

Recent studies have expressed concern at the lack of some of these essential fatty acids in the diets of pregnant vegetarian women. Omega-6 fats are found in olive oil and sunflower oil, while the omega-3 fatty acids are abundant in oily fish, soybean and canola oil, and walnuts.

✚ *Vital for development of the brain and the central nervous system.*
✚ *Best eaten as olive, sunflower, and canola oil, oily fish, soybeans, and walnuts*

## TRANS FATS
*Harmful in excess*

Trans fats are not listed or food labels, although you may occasionally find a margarine that declares itself to be free of, or low in, trans fats. After decades of being told that margarines are safer for your heart than butter, American research points the finger directly at these previously ignored culprits.

Liquid oils go through a process called hydrogenation in order to convert them into solid or semisolid margarines. Commercial cooking oils are also partially hydrogenated, which gives them a longer life in the deep-fat fryer and so makes them commercially attractive. A byproduct of this process are the trans fats, and enormous population studies in the United States have revealed that these trans fats are as bad as, and possibly worse than, saturated fats as a cause of serious heart disease.

➖ *Best avoided in direct form.*
➖ *Linked with heart disease.*

## CHOLESTEROL

Cholesterol levels in the blood are a key marker of an individual's risk of heart disease. Though other factors are involved—such as smoking, obesity, lack of exercise, and overall diet—cholesterol is of fundamental importance. It is an essential constituent of every cell in the body, but we do not need to consume cholesterol, because we actually manufacture it from other fats.

▶ Most people with raised blood-cholesterol levels can reduce them by cutting down on the amount of saturated fat in their diet, whereas lowering the intake of dietary cholesterol itself benefits only a small percentage of those with raised levels. There is no cholesterol in plant foods, but it is found in all animal and animal-based foods, the highest amount being present in organ meats and egg yolk.

▶ There are two ways in which cholesterol circulates in the body. It is attached either to Low-Density Lipoproteins (LDLs) or High-Density Lipoproteins (HDLs). LDLs are the bad guys (remember: L = lethal) and it is people with high levels of LDL circulating in their bloodstreams that are at the highest risk of heart disease. Heavy consumption of saturated animal fat increases the amount of LDLs. High levels of HDL in the blood, however, signify a reduced risk of heart disease.

▶ High-cholesterol foods that contain little other saturated fat seem to make very little difference to blood-cholesterol levels. But there are many foods, especially those high in soluble fiber, such as oatmeal, dried fruit, and grapefruit, that encourage the body to eliminate surplus cholesterol. Food labelled "cholesterol-free" or "low in cholesterol" can be very misleading; it is the percentage of saturated fat that you should look out for.

## BUTTER

*Energy per standard portion 74 calories*
*Rich in vitamins A, D, and E*

This is delicious and, in modest use, it is certainly better for you than nearly all margarines, since butter is a natural product and margarine the synthetic product of a factory. The bad news is that it is virtually all fat, and 60 percent of that comprises saturated fat. 3½oz/100g of butter provides 740 calories, but it is a rich source of vitamins A, D, and E. Some brands are much higher in salt than others—it may contain anything from no salt at all to 1300mg per 3½oz/100g. In Britain, butter may be colored but may not contain antioxidants, unless the finished product is exclusively for manufacturing or catering use.

Unlike most other dairy products, butter is a poor source of calcium and contains virtually no B vitamins at all.

- ✚ *Provides essential fatty acids for healthy skin and development of body cells.*
- ✚ *Best used modestly, even sparingly, instead of margarine.*
- ➖ *Do not put butter on burns or scalds—the heat from the wound causes the butter to fry.*

## MARGARINE

*Energy per standard portion 74 calories*
*Rich in vitamins D and E*

Margarine is a complex chemical product combining oils, fats, flavoring, and coloring made by a process first invented by the French chemist Mège Mouries in Paris in 1869. It is usually a blend of vegetable, animal, or fish oils, which hydrogenation converts from liquid to solid or soft margarine. This is the process that produces the harmful trans fats as a byproduct. The total amount of fat in all but low-fat spreads is about the same in margarines as it is in butter. But while 3½oz/100g of butter provides 2oz/54g of saturated fat, hard margarines contain only 1¼oz/36g and polyunsaturated margarines only ½oz/16g.

Low-fat spreads are much lower in calories and fats and, similar to polyunsaturated margarines, are cholesterol-free. Remember, though, that cholesterol-free does not mean fat-free.

- ✚ *Provides essential fatty acids for healthy skin and development of body cells.*
- ➖ *Best replaced by a little butter.*

## VEGETABLE OILS

❸

*Energy per standard portion 99 calories*
*Rich in vitamin E*

Like all fats, oils are enormous providers of calories—899 per 3½oz/100g. Most vegetable oils contain little saturated fat and good supplies of vitamin E; palm and coconut oil, however, both contain large amounts of saturated fat and coconut oil virtually no vitamin E. It is likely that either of these oils will be a constituent of anything labeled "vegetable oil," so make sure that you avoid buying this. The polyunsaturated fats in vegetable oils are extremely important because they contain essential fatty acids that our bodies do not make for themselves. Sunflower is the richest of all in vitamin E, containing 49µg per 3½oz/100g of oil.

Sunflower, corn, and safflower oils are ideal for light salad dressings and for cooking. Specialty oils like walnut, soybean, and sesame seed have come to the fore in recent years with the increased interest in stir-frying. Almond oil is good for salad dressings, and canola oil (rapeseed) has very little flavor but is useful for frying as it has a high smoke point. Hazelnut oil has a distinctive flavor but a low smoke point—good for sauces, but not for frying. Peanut (groundnut) oil has a distinctive nutty flavor and a high smoke point, is low in saturated and high in monounsaturated fats, and has a reasonable amount of polyunsaturateds. It makes a good all-purpose oil.

➕ *Provides essential fatty acids for healthy skin and development of body cells.*
➕ *Best used in salad dressings or for stir-frying, when little of the oil is absorbed by the food.*
➖ *It is a serious health hazard to overheat or repeatedly use the same oil for frying food; this results in the production of toxic chemicals.*

### FAST FOOD FACT

● Use vegetable oil or olive oil as an emollient to soothe very dry skin or psoriasis. These oils are most effective if you apply them after a bath.

## OLIVE OIL

❶ ❷ ❸ ❹ ❺

*Energy per standard portion 99 calories*
*Rich in vitamin E*

Scientific research has now confirmed the peasant wisdom of the Mediterranean area that olive oil is a marvelous food-medicine. One of the most powerful antioxidants is vitamin E, and olive oil is lavishly supplied with the most active—alpha—form of this vitamin. It actually has antioxidant activity to spare, and generous amounts of the best-quality olive oil can be consumed without risk. Olive oil is now considered to have a protective effect against maladies in which free-radical activity is implicated, among them cancer, arthritis, premature senility, and cardiovascular disease. Regular olive-oil eaters also have more beneficial HDLs, possibly contributing to the heart-protective effect of the Mediterranean diet.

Recent research has shown that the bile-promoting effect of olive oil is both more intense and longer-lasting than that of other fats. This explains why, on a digestibility rating of 100 set up by the US Food and Drug Administration, olive oil scored full marks, sunflower oil 83, peanut oil 81, and corn oil only 36. It is also more efficiently absorbed and promotes intestinal peristalsis to carry food through the body; it is therefore the friend of the liverish, the dyspeptic and the ulcer victim.

➕ *Protective against cancer, heart disease, ulcers, and arthritis.*

➕ *Best used as extra-virgin olive oil, in which the vital antioxidants are preserved; but it is wasted used for frying, because its delicate flavor is destroyed in the process.*

### FAST FOOD FACT

● For dry, brittle, and perm-damaged hair, olive oil makes a superb deep-conditioning treatment. Comb the oil into wet or damp hair, cover with plastic wrap, then wrap up in a towel; leave for a couple of hours, then shampoo as normal.

# SWEET FOODS
# AND DRINKS

*Sweet foods*

*Tea and coffee*

*Water*

*Alcohol*

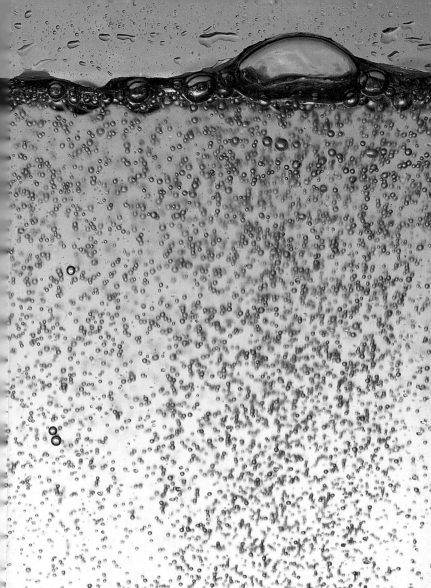

# SWEET FOODS AND DRINKS

Sugar supplies energy, but contains no useful nutrients. And we can get all the energy we need from healthier sources, such as fruit, vegetables, and milk. Drinks, on the other hand, are vital to maintain the body's correct fluid balance, but we should concentrate on the healing powers of water, rather than sugar-laden beverages.

ROUGH SUGAR

A diet in which a high proportion of the energy content comes from refined sugars (sugary drinks, snacks, confectionery) tends to be low in vitamins, minerals, and dietary fiber. Consumption of refined sugars in the United States and Europe now supplies an average of 14–17 percent of energy, with some children consuming even higher amounts of around 17–20 percent. The worrying thing is that this pattern is now being repeated in other parts of the world, with increasing industrialization.

HONEY

Soft drinks, candies, cakes, and cookies are frequently heavily advertised, widely available, and promoted as more desirable than healthier alternatives. They tend to be the foods we snack on, which fill us up so that we are not hungry for more nutritious foods at mealtimes; they cause

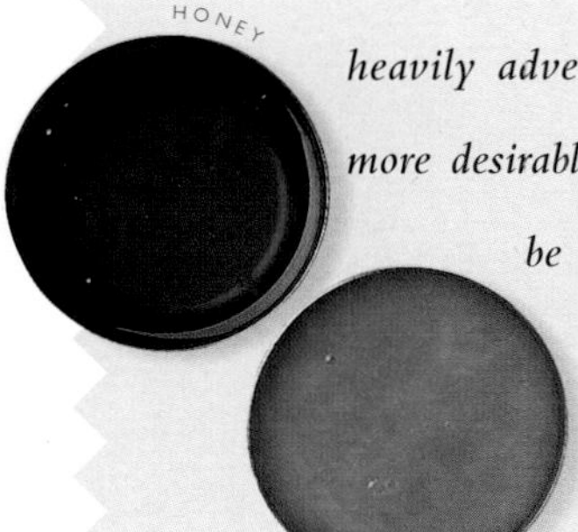

tooth decay and can lead to obesity, since often
we do not realize that we are eating more
energy than the body actually needs.

Our seemingly insatiable sweet tooth
has prompted soft-drink manufacturers to
produce and aggressively market a wide range of drinks
containing high amounts of sugar and flavorings; or
sweeteners, to satisfy those who want to cut down on the
calories. Sweeteners are also used in many prepared
foods. While manufacturers claim that sweeteners are
safe, some of them have been withdrawn from the market
because of their links with cancer, and the effects of long-
term use are hard to determine.

Since water makes up 50–70 percent
of an adult's body weight, it is important
that we drink enough to satisfy our
thirst and to keep body fluid in balance.
Drinking can also help to relieve
constipation. Water, tea, and coffee are
still the most popular sources of fluid—though tea and
coffee contain insignificant amounts of nutrients, they are
drunk mainly for their refreshing taste and their
stimulant activity; but water is still the healthiest option,
as long as it comes from a clean source.

WHITE SUGAR

DEMERERA SUGAR

# SUGAR

BROWN SUGAR
*Energy per 3 1/2 oz / 100g 362 calories*

WHITE SUGAR
*Energy per 3 1/2 oz / 100g 394 calories*
*Nutritionally poor*

The sugar you buy in your local store, whether it is white or brown, is not natural or good for you. Sugar will not directly cause a heart attack, diabetes, behavioral disturbances, or acne, but it is often the first link in an inevitably progressive chain that leads to health disasters. Reducing the total sugar consumption by 50 percent in the United States and Britain would have an enormous impact on health.

A regular diet that supplies too much refined sugar can lead to a condition known as hypoglycemia, where there is, in fact, too little sugar present in the blood. This may be caused by diabetes or by a disease of the pancreas, but is often the result of bad eating habits. Sweating, shaking, faintness, dizziness, headaches, and confusion can all develop when your blood-sugar level is too low.

Refined sugar, an essential ingredient of so many jams, cakes, puddings, cookies, canned fruits, and soft drinks, contains absolutely no nutritional value—all you get is a large

helping of calories and rotten teeth. And there is now a growing suspicion that poor eating habits, irregular meals, and a high sugar intake may seriously damage your state of mind. Depression, fatigue, irritability, poor concentration, PMS, mood swings, poor performance at school, and hyperactivity are just some of the conditions that can be improved by eating better food, timing meals with more care, and reducing the consumption of refined sugars.

The average consumption of sugar in Britain is around 2lb/1kg per head each week—or more than 100lb/45kg a year for every man, woman, and child. Since adults tend to consume fewer high-sugar foods, just think how much sugar most children are eating. Most of it comes from soft drinks, candies, and chocolate bars, and large quantities of processed food, and the hidden sugar in many manufactured products is alarming.

Sugar represents very poor nutritional value for money and is frequently used as a cheap bulking ▶

198

ROUGH SUGAR

MOLASSES

**sugar continued**

agent in highly processed convenience foods, so replacing more nourishing produce with empty calories. It is also known to increase the amount of triglyceride fats excreted from the sebaceous glands of the skin, so I am in no doubt that the first step to better skin is a reduction in sugar.

White sugar is bad for you, but brown sugar is good—true or false? Although unrefined sugars are marginally less bad for you, their minute quantities of nutrients are usually absorbed from the processing machinery. Honey contains tiny traces

of nutrients and has other healing properties, but it is 20 percent water. Maple, corn, and glucose syrups, fructose, and maltose are all sugars under the guise of different names.

➕ *Best eaten very sparingly.*

➖ *Excess refined sugar can cause hypoglycemia and exacerbate fatigue, depression, and mood swings.*

➖ *Excessive sugar consumption can increase the risk of cholesterol deposits in the arteries; those most at risk are men, some women on the contraceptive pill, and women past the menopause.*

## HIDDEN SUGAR

| FOOD | TEASPOONS OF SUGAR |
|------|--------------------|
| One plain Graham cracker | 0.5 |
| Modest portion of baked beans | 1 |
| One chocolate Graham cracker | 1 |
| One plain donut | 1 |
| One scoop of plain ice-cream | 2 |
| Three teaspoons of jam | 2.5 |
| Average slice of cake | 3 |
| Average portion of sugar-frosted breakfast cereal | 3 |
| Three teaspoons of honey | 3 |
| Average fruit yogurt | 4.5 |
| 11fl oz/330ml can of soda | 7 |
| Medium-size can of fruit in syrup | 10 |
| 3½oz/100g bar of chocolate | 11 |
| 3½oz/100g pack of hard candies or peppermints | 18 |

GRANULATED SWEETENER

## SWEETENERS

*Energy per standard portion 0 calories*
*Nutritionally poor*

Artificial sweeteners crop up everywhere: in ordinary foods—potato chips, candies, medicines, sauces, and even savory dishes—as well as in "low-calorie" products. Surprisingly there is little evidence that they help you consume fewer calories, although it is true that artificial sweeteners—saccharin, acesulfame-K, and aspartame— contain no calories themselves. There are also bulk sweeteners—mannitol, xylitol, sorbitol—which are used as bulking agents in many processed foods. They do not contain sucrose but do provide about the same number of calories as ordinary sugar. Their advantage is that they do not cause dental decay, so they are often found in candies and chewing gums that carry the "tooth-friendly" label. They can, however, cause diarrhea if they are taken in excessive amounts.

Artificial sweeteners act just like natural sugars, by stimulating the sweet-sensitive tastebuds on the tongue. Saccharin, for example, is 400 times sweeter than sugar, so tiny amounts can make things taste very sweet indeed. Unfortunately, it also leaves a bitter metallic aftertaste.

Few manufacturers reveal the actual amounts of sweetener in their products, and it is not even clear how much of the chemical is in the sweeteners you drop into your coffee or tea. The safe amount of saccharin for a girl of $6\frac{1}{2}$ weighing 44lb/20kg to consume each day would be 100mg. The British Consumers' Association magazine *Which?* calculates that a couple of glasses of orange drink, a strawberry ice cream cone, a glass of sugar-free lemon drink, a can of sugar-free cola, an individual trifle, a portion of reduced-sugar baked beans, and a package of shrimp-flavored potato chips would give her an over-the-limit total of 112mg.

Dr. Michael Jacobson, Director of the Center for Science in the Public Interest (CSPI) in Washington, DC, has serious reservations about their safety. A number of studies during the 1970s linked saccharine with cancer in laboratory animals and the government subsequently took it off the list of safe chemicals and finally banned it in 1977. Saccharin was eventually exempted from the American food-safety laws and is now regarded as safe by government ▶

SWEETENER TABLETS

*sweeteners continued*

scientists in Britain, although in the United States foods containing saccharin have to carry a warning label that indicates their cancer-causing effect on laboratory animals!

Dr. Jacobson has called for a ban on acesulfame-K in the United States, and the CSPI considers it the worst culprit. It claims that this sweetener is inadequately tested and that tests show that it causes cancer in animals, which means that it may increase the risk for humans. Government experts admitted that the safety data were not ideal but decided that there was enough evidence to prove its safety.

Aspartame poses some very specific problems. One of its ingredients is phenylalanine, a natural component of proteins. One in 20,000 babies is born with an illness called phenylketonuria (PKU—remember your baby's pricked heel test) and is not able to break down phenylalanine. Raised levels of this chemical can cause brain damage and retardation. For this reason all products containing aspartame carry the warning, "Contains phenylalanine." Government scientists maintain the product to be safe but some experts believe that a high intake could pose a risk to the babies of pregnant women who carry the trait for PKU. Jacobson says, "Many people (though a minuscule fraction of those who have consumed the additive) have reported dizziness, headaches, epileptic-like seizures, and menstrual problems after ingesting aspartame."

Cyclamate is currently banned in the United States after tests showed an increase of cancer in laboratory animals fed on it. In Britain, it was reapproved in January 1996, and so cyclamates came back onto the market.

- *Best avoided.*
- *Linked with cancer in animals.*
- *Avoid sweeteners if you are pregnant; and do not give them to children.*

## CHOCOLATE

❹ ❺

MILK CHOCOLATE
*Energy per 3¹⁄₂oz / 100g 520 calories*
*Rich in protein and some minerals*

Both chocolate and cocoa are made from cocoa beans. Cocoa is made by grinding the beans to a paste, adding sugar and starch, and removing the fat. For chocolate, most of the fat is left in and its quality is determined by the percentage of cocoa solids in the finished product: at least 50 percent for "quality chocolate," but for the very best this rises to 70 percent. The fat, known as cocoa butter, is very soothing to the skin and is widely used in the manufacture of cosmetics and in the pharmaceutical trade.

In spite of its high fat content, chocolate is quite nutritious, dark chocolate especially being a good source of iron and magnesium. Chocolate supplies useful amounts of protein, traces of other minerals, and some of the B vitamins, but it is loaded with calories.

You would need to walk briskly for two hours, pedal your bicycle for an hour and half, or swim nonstop for an hour in order to burn off the 520 calories contained in a 3¹⁄₂oz/100g bar of chocolate.

➕ *Dilates the blood vessels, so can also be useful in the treatment of high blood pressure.*
➕ *Beneficial for depression, because of its theobromine content.*
➕ *Best eaten in moderation.*
➖ *The caffeine in chocolate may trigger migraine attacks.*

### SUPER FOOD

● Modest amounts of chocolate can give the depressive a real lift, since it contains the chemical theobromine, which is believed to trigger the release of natural "feel-good" chemicals in the brain, and it is these endorphins that also kindle the feelings of romance, love, and arousal. Theobromine also has a stimulating effect on the heart muscle and kidneys and was traditionally used by medical herbalists, with the plant *Digitalis*, for fluid retention linked to heart failure.

## LICORICE

❷ ❹ ❻

*Energy per standard portion 4 calories*
*Rich in glycyrrhizic acid and iron*

Although most people think of licorice as a commercially produced candy, it is in fact a powerful antiinflammatory, which works in the same way as hydrocortisone. It is the root of the licorice plant that is valuable, containing glycyrrhizic acid, a chemical 50 times sweeter than sugar. Powdered licorice root contains a large amount of iron, so licorice confectionery supplies over 8mg of this essential mineral per 3½oz/100g

This herb is an effective laxative. For the treatment of constipation put ¾oz/20g of dried licorice stick in 3½ cups/750ml of cold water, bring to a boil, and simmer until reduced by one-third; strain into a pitcher, cover, and refrigerate, then drink a cupful each morning and evening.

➕ *Good for coughs, digestive problems (especially ulcers), liver problems, anemia, arthritis, and nausea.*
➕ *Best eaten as pastilles or sticks.*
➖ *Taking large doses for long periods can cause high blood pressure; pregnant women and those with high blood pressure should avoid it.*

## HONEY

❶ ❷ ❼

*Energy per standard portion 49 calories*
*Rich in fructose and glucose*

In impressive clinical trials, manuka honey from New Zealand has been shown to be an excellent remedy for the treatment of stomach ulcers. Two teaspoons after each meal and at bedtime for a month can eliminate all traces of *Helicobacter pylori*—a major cause of gastric ulcers. And for sore throats and chesty coughs, honey is a sovereign remedy. Mixed with hot water and lemon juice, it is soothing and an effective expectorant.

➕ *Beneficial for coughs, sore throats, stomach ulcers, and even leg ulcers.*
➕ *Best used as a substitute for sugar in recipes or as a soothing drink.*

### FAST FOOD FACT

● Natural honey, unlike the product of sugar-fed bees and commercial honey, has some extraordinary healing powers. Used postoperatively on sterile dressings, it speeds up healing and reduces scarring. Spread on gauze and used on varicose leg ulcers, honey can stimulate the healing process.

# DRINKS

*Prized for their refreshing, stimulant effect*

COFFEE BEAN

Tea has been cultivated in China for over 2,000 years. It first appeared in Britain during the seventeenth century and remained an expensive luxury for some time. It probably owes its popularity to its refreshing and stimulating effect (due to the presence of caffeine), as well as to the appetizing, delicate aroma of the volatile oil that it contains. Teas made from various herbs or fruits are now gaining in popularity in many countries as refreshing alternatives to ordinary black tea.

Coffee is made from coffee beans, the dried seeds of the fruit of the coffee bush, which is grown primarily in Latin America, Africa, and Indonesia. It purportedly originated in Persia and was introduced to Aden in the fifteenth century. Green coffee beans are roasted by one of several methods, then ground; the best-flavored coffee is obtained from beans that are ground just before use.

Both coffee and tea contain fairly small amounts of vitamins and minerals, but do contain biologically active

ASSAM TEA

substances, including caffeine, flavonoids, and phenols. These are now being studied (particularly the last two) for their possible anticarcinogenic properties; but the negative associations of caffeine should also be recognized. Some soft drinks also contain caffeine.

COMFREY TEA

ASSAM TEA

CAMOMILE TEA

## TEA

❶ ❷ ❹

*Energy per standard portion—trace*
*Rich in vitamins E and K*

Tea is almost certainly the most popular of all drinks worldwide. In the West it is most common to drink black tea, which is the fermented leaf of the Indian tea plant. Green tea, largely drunk in Japan and China, is not fermented, is drunk without milk or sugar and produces a pale, greenish-yellow-colored liquid.

Tea has long been credited with health benefits. Its caffeine content is about half that of coffee, making tea a mild stimulant, which helps to revive the flagging spirits. Black tea supplies important amounts of vitamins E and K, and small amounts of the B vitamins. Tea also contains some very interesting phenolic compounds, and research in Russia and eastern Europe has shown that these chemicals can strengthen the walls of the tiniest capillary blood vessels.

Tea is also a good source of the important trace elements manganese and fluorine, and contains the astringent substance known as tannin (though green teas have much less of this than black teas). Tannins have an antibacterial effect and may help in the treatment of stomach infections.

But it is the antioxidant and cancer-protective effects of the bioflavonoids in tea that are the most exciting discoveries. There is growing evidence that populations consuming large amounts of green tea have a lower incidence of heart disease and of some forms of cancer. This also now appears to be true, although to a slightly lesser extent, of black tea.

➕ *A mild stimulant for those suffering from fatigue and exhaustion.*

➕ *A good cancer-protector, and beneficial for the heart.*

➕ *Best drunk with either milk or lemon, or iced.*

➖ *The tannins in tea can interfere with the body's uptake of essential minerals, especially iron, and those who drink a lot of strong tea are at risk of anemia.*

➖ *Can be an irritant to those suffering from stomach ulcers.*

GROUND COFFEE

INSTANT COFFEE

COFFEE BEANS

## COFFEE

**②** **⑤** **⑦**

BLACK COFFEE
*Energy per standard portion 4 calories*
*Rich in caffeine and niacin*

Caffeine is a brain stimulant and can be of value in the treatment of narcotic poisoning, while temporary improvements in awareness can be valuable at times of extreme exhaustion. Caffeine can be useful for some asthmatics, since it is quite similar to theophylline, an effective antiasthma drug. It also increases the effectiveness of some everyday painkillers and is often included in proprietary formulations. And caffeine is used medicinally to restrict blood flow to the brain as part of antimigraine medication. In Indian Ayurvedic medicine the coffee bean has a long history of use for the treatment of diarrhea and for headaches.

But while there are positive uses of caffeine, it is important to weigh up the risk/benefit associations, since coffee drinking is implicated in a number of serious health problems.

More than five or six cups a day can lead to caffeinism, or coffee addiction. Coffee affects the blood pressure, and avoidance for a few weeks can reduce both systolic and diastolic pressures. PMS and cyclic breast lumps are said to improve by avoiding coffee, and consistent and large quantities of coffee can increase a woman's chances of osteoporosis. Three cups of coffee per day may reduce a woman's chances of conception and increase the risk of miscarriage, low birth-weight babies, and birth defects.

Smokers actually eliminate caffeine from their bodies twice as quickly as nonsmokers. To maintain their heightened sense of awareness they need to drink twice as much coffee.

➕ *Good for stimulation when tired.*
➕ *Helpful for fluid retention, asthma, headaches, and diarrhea.*
➕ *Best drunk filtered and in very small quantities.*
➖ *Caffeine can interfere with mineral absorption, and increase the insulin produced by the pancreas, leading to hypoglycemia; it can also seriously affect the digestive system.*
➖ *May exacerbate PMS, raised blood pressure, osteoporosis, the risk of miscarriage, and birth problems.*

# WATER

*Prized for its mineral content*
*and cleansing properties*

Water is one of the most powerful, and easily available, of all medicines. Used by people in the form of hot and cold springs, sulfur springs, as sea water, river and mountain water, it has provided external as well as internal therapy for centuries. Most important of all is the water we drink—and few people drink enough. Kidney problems, cystitis, migraine, headaches, skin disorders, and constipation may all have their roots in a lack of fluid intake.

Mineral waters not only taste good, but have health-giving properties as well. The bottles that we buy today contain rain water that fell up to 80 years ago and has been filtered through layers of purifying sand, shale, and rock, enriching the water with natural minerals—the most beneficial of which are calcium (for building bones) and magnesium (to increase the body's resistance to disease). If you are suffering from digestive problems, then water containing more of the minerals would certainly help.

But taste is also a major factor. In areas of low rainfall, leading to major hygiene problems in the water industry, and with chemical accidents at purifying plants and the uncertainty of supply, mineral waters look a lot more appetizing, especially when you realize that nearly all tap water is recycled, and if you live in London, New York, or any other big city, yours could well be the seventh pair of kidneys that your glass of water has passed through!

WATER

## SPRING AND TABLE WATER

② ③ ⑤ ⑧

*Energy per standard portion 4 calories*
*No particular properties*

These may come from a spring or out of a tap connected to your local water supply. As long as the contents of the bottle meet the same standards as those required for tap water, bottling companies can virtually do what they like. They need not identify the source of the water. They can mix water from different sources, filter it, disinfect it, and put very little information on the label.

✛ *Best drunk refrigerated and before its sell-by date.*
➖ *Anyone with high blood pressure or heart disease should avoid waters with a high sodium content.*

## MINERAL WATER

② ③ ⑤ ⑧

*Energy per standard portion 4 calories*
*Rich in calcium, magnesium,*
*and sodium*

Mineral water must come from a single underground source and be free of dangerous bacteria and polluting chemicals. Its mineral content must always be the same, and although the water can be filtered and exposed to ultraviolet light, no other sterilizing or disinfecting process is allowed. Water can be naturally gassy when it comes out of the ground and this fizziness can be increased by carbon dioxide, or reduced by mechanical methods. Mineral water must be bottled at, or very close to, its source. The label must always indicate the mineral content and there are strict conditions governing the use of terms such as "low mineral content," "rich in mineral salts," and "suitable for a low-sodium diet."

✛ *Good for kidney problems, cystitis, headaches and migraines, skin complaints, and constipation.*
✛ *Best drunk refrigerated and before its sell-by date.*
➖ *Anyone with high blood pressure or heart disease should avoid mineral water with a high sodium content.*

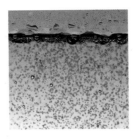

## RESTAURANT BOTTLED WATER

② ③ ⑤ ⑧

*Energy per standard portion 4 calories*
*No particular properties*

Some restaurant chains are making enormous profits by stocking only their own in-house bottled water. This may be nothing more than tap water that has been through a plumbed-in filtration system to remove the taste of chlorine and some of the minerals. You're probably better off asking for a large pitcher of iced water and giving it a good stir to remove some of the excessive chlorine.

➕ *Best drunk refrigerated and before its sell-by date.*

➖ *Anyone with high blood pressure or heart disease should avoid waters with a high sodium content.*

### SPAS

The art of hydrotherapy—using showers, baths of different temperatures, steam, and alternate hot and cold bathing—has been part of the history of healing over many centuries. In the nineteenth century, people flocked to Bath, Buxton, Leamington, Cheltenham, and Harrogate in Britain, to Evian, Vichy, Baden-Baden, and Sangermini in Europe, and to Hot Springs Calistoga, Saratoga Springs, and Poland Spring in the United States, in order to take the waters. Now, 100 years later, we are rediscovering their taste and value, and the huge rise in the popularity of mineral waters has helped make people more aware of water, which we so often take for granted.

## VOLVIC
*Plain*

This mountain water, from the deserted volcanic region of the Auvergne, takes many years to drain through the basalt rocks. It is best drunk chilled and is good for making up baby foods and for skin problems.

| | |
|---|---|
| Source | *Clairvic Spring, France* |
| Calcium content (mg/l) | *9.9* |
| Magnesium content (mg/l) | *6.1* |
| Sodium content (mg/l) | *9.4* |
| Total mineral content | *low* |
| Taste | *very plain, hardly flavored water* |

## VICHY
*Naturally fizzy*

The most fashionable and elegant of all the spas in the 1800s, Vichy was frequented by Napoleon III and most of the crowned heads of Europe. It is the water for digestive problems, rheumatism, and kidney stones.

| | |
|---|---|
| Source | *Vichy, France* |
| Calcium content (mg/l) | *100* |
| Magnesium content (mg/l) | *9* |
| Sodium content (mg/l) | *1,200* |
| Total mineral content | *high* |
| Taste | *very alkaline, very slightly fizzy* |

## EVIAN
*Plain*

The spa at Evian has been famous since the eighteenth century for the treatment of kidney stones and urinary infections. Evian water takes 15 years to filter down from the alpine snows to the spring in the town.

| | |
|---|---|
| Source | *Evian, Lake Geneva, France* |
| Calcium content (mg/l) | *78* |
| Magnesium content (mg/l) | *24* |
| Sodium content (mg/l) | *5* |
| Total mineral content | *low* |
| Taste | *pure, very clean taste* |

## SAN PELLEGRINO
*Carbonated*

Leonardo da Vinci drank this water plain, very warm, and with its metallic aftertaste, just as it came straight from the spring. Modern carbonated water loses most of the mineral flavor, which is replaced by a sparkling crispness.

| | |
|---|---|
| Source | *Italian Alps* |
| Calcium content (mg/l) | *203* |
| Magnesium content (mg/l) | *56.9* |
| Sodium content (mg/l) | *46.5* |
| Total mineral content | *medium* |
| Taste | *a refreshing, distinctive flavor* |

## MOUNTAIN VALLEY SPRING
*Plain and carbonated*

This is the American equivalent of the great spas of Europe, its waters revered for their healing properties by the native North Americans. Theodore Roosevelt was a regular visitor, and the purity of the water was unrivaled.

| | |
|---|---|
| Source | *Hot Springs National Park, Arkansas* |
| Calcium content (mg/l) | *68* |
| Magnesium content (mg/l) | *8* |
| Sodium content (mg/l) | *2.8* |
| Total mineral content | *low* |
| Taste | *very slightly alkaline* |

## POLAND SPRING
*Plain and carbonated*

This water filters through fine sand and gravel deposited 10,000 years ago by moving glaciers and is exceptionally pure, with a mineral content totaling only 46mg/l. Originally promoted at the turn of the nineteenth century.

| | |
|---|---|
| Source | *Poland Spring, Maine* |
| Calcium content (mg/l) | *nil* |
| Magnesium content (mg/l) | *1.6* |
| Sodium content (mg/l) | *3* |
| Total mineral content | *very low* |
| Taste | *very clean* |

# ALCOHOL

There is no physiological need for alcohol, and alcohol is an addictive drug; but for many people drinking alcohol is a pleasant social activity.

Alcohol is produced by the fermentation of sources of carbohydrate, including grapes and other fruit, grains, roots, and cacti. Very many different types of alcoholic drinks are made and consumed around the world, but most fall into the three

broad categories of beers, wines, and spirits (liquor). Consumption of alcohol differs in different parts of the world—and even within countries—from zero to around 10 percent of total energy. But individuals may consume far more, and alcohol is a major public-health problem.

Alcohol is used by the body as an energy source; but if more than the recommended number of units is consumed it can often take the place of nutritious foods and interfere with the metabolism of some nutrients. Beer is a source of B vitamins, except thiamin, but the amounts vary in different beers.

Consumption of alcohol at low levels is believed to reduce the risk of coronary heart disease. On the other hand, there is evidence that alcohol increases the risk of certain cancers, notably of the mouth and pharynx, larynx, and esophagus. For your health's sake buy the best quality you can afford, and drink less of it.

## BEER
④ ⑤ ⑧

*Energy per $\frac{1}{2}$pt/330ml 70–125 calories*
*Rich in vitamin $B_{12}$*

Energy is mostly what you get from beer—anything from 70 to 125 calories in each half-pint. All beers contain alcohol but no protein and, with the exception of potassium, beer contains virtually no other minerals. It is, however, an exceptionally good source of vitamin $B_{12}$.

There are great differences between a traditionally brewed real beer and the lagers and keg bitters. Barley is first sprouted and then malted. The resulting "wort" is boiled with hops (rich in a number of resins, which impart the unique flavor to beer) and then brewer's yeast is added to start the fermentation process. Stouts are generally sweeter because of their higher sugar content; ordinary lagers contain slightly less alcohol than beer or stout. Traditional British cask beers are brewed in the old-fashioned manner without chemical additives, kept in wooden barrels, and lifted from the cellar by manual pumps. In much of Europe and the United States, the taste is for lighter, more gaseous beers and lagers, but these can cause bloating and abdominal discomfort.

Unfortunately, the idea that stout is highly nutritious is a myth. Nonetheless, in modest quantities beer is an effective diuretic and a good source of vitamin $B_{12}$ and energy, which helps with anemia, lethargy, and Tired-All-The-Time syndrome (TATT).

➕ *Good for anemia, TATT (but not ME), and fluid retention.*

➕ *Best drunk at cellar temperature, if it is real ale; however, most people seem to prefer an ice-cold beer—perhaps the coldness disguises its lack of flavor.*

### FAST FOOD FACT

● To add a really good luster to dull, lifeless hair, rinse it with beer after first shampooing thoroughly. This helps the cuticles on the hair shaft lie flat to give you a glossy mane. Alternatively, beer shampoos are available commercially.

WHITE WINE

RED WINE

# WINE

❹

RED WINE
*Energy per standard glass 85 calories*

WHITE WINE
*Energy per standard glass 93 calories*
*Rich in easily absorbed iron*

There is still some controversy over the benefits of wine drinking, but it does now seem clear that *modest* intakes can have a significant benefit in terms of reduced heart and circulatory disease. Most medical experts agree that consumption should not exceed 14 units per week for women and 21 units per week for men, a unit being one measure of spirits, one small glass of wine, or half a pint of normal beer or cider.

Though most wine is made from grapes, all countries have a tradition of making wine from other forms of fresh produce—elderberries, gooseberries, rhubarb, parsnips, apples, or almost any other fruit or vegetable with a reasonable sugar content. Commercial wine production from grapes often includes a number of chemical substances, some of which can cause health problems. Colorings, flavorings, and preservatives may also be added, and there is normally no requirement for

wine makers to declare these on the label. Sulfur dioxide, for instance, a common preservative in wines, is a frequent trigger of asthma in susceptible people. And substances known as congeners in red wine are suspected of triggering migraine. In general, the cheaper the wine, the more chemicals it will contain and the worse your hangover will be.

Although the amounts of iron in both red and white wine are fairly small—around 1mg in an average glass—they are extremely well absorbed. Indeed, alcoholics, who frequently have a low-protein diet, may absorb so much iron from alcohol that it causes serious liver damage.

➕ *Good for cardiovascular protection, improving the circulation, mild depression, and anemia.*

➕ *Best drunk in moderation—the above benefits depend on modest consumptions only; larger quantities have the reverse effect.*

➖ *May trigger asthma or migraine.*

# VITAMINS AND MINERALS

I always ask my patients to bring any supplements that they are taking when they come to see me. Lots of them turn up with plastic bags full of them! This really upsets me, because they are certainly spending too much money on them and some vitamins and minerals can be dangerous if taken in high doses.

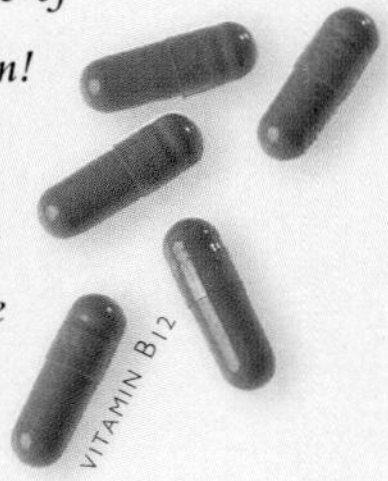

VITAMIN B12

The American recommended daily allowances (RDAs) for vitamins and minerals are generally higher than those in Britain; however, I am concerned about both sets of RDAs. Governments make no allowance for the huge variations in the actual nutrient content of today's foods. Intensive growing methods, transporting, storing, handling, and freshness can all reduce the level of vitamins in food. And that is before you buy them, take them home, and cook them. The theoretical vitamin content of what ends up on your plate is often a great deal higher than the reality of what you acutally put into your mouth.

ZINC CAPSULES

There is also an enormous difference between the amount of vitamins and minerals you need in order to avoid deficiency diseases and those that will keep you in peak condition and protect your body against serious illness. On the pages that follow are details of what some of the vitamins and minerals actually do (together with cautions concerning excessive intakes), what the best food sources are, and the current RDAs.

## VITAMINS

The burning question most people ask is, "Do I need to take extra vitamins?" The theoretical answer is no—not if you are eating a well-balanced diet and getting a wide variety of foods. In fact, few people manage this.

Natural health insurance, in the form of an inexpensive, well-formulated multivitamin and mineral pill, can be a good idea. It will make up for the occasional missed meal, the extra demands of a stressful life, the vitamin losses during storage, transportation, and cooking of food, and will buoy you up after an illness.

Read the labels carefully, and avoid pills with artificial colors, flavorings, and preservatives. Watch out for added sugar or sweeteners.

Many children, especially those with asthma, eczema, or other allergy problems, and hyperactive children, react badly to many of the food chemicals in some vitamin pills.

On the other hand, some manufacturers are cashing in on the "allergy" syndrome and making expensive products that are gluten-, yeast-, egg-, milk-, and everything-else-free. Unless you know that you are allergic to certain foods—and comparatively few people are—there is no need to go to these lengths.

Choose multivitamins with substantial levels of the main nutrients, rather than huge lists of nutrients you have never heard of. Adult formulations are not normally suitable for children from the ages of two to ten, who should be given the relevant products. Children under two

| RECOMMENDED DAILY ALLOWANCES | |
|---|---|
| RDAs from the Food and Drug Administration | |
| A | 5,000IU |
| C | 60mg |
| D | 400IU |
| E | 30IU |
| Thiamin | 1.5mg |
| Riboflavin | 1.7mg |
| Niacin | 20mg |
| $B_6$ | 2.0mg |
| $B_{12}$ | 6.0µg |
| Folate | 0.4mg |
| Biotin | 0.3mg |
| Pantothenic acid | 10mg |

µg = microgram
IU = International Units

should take supplements only on professional advice. Beware of taking excessive amounts of vitamins, which can cause serious health problems.

Single supplements do have a place in the treatment and prevention of certain conditions—for instance, extra vitamin C as protection against colds and infections during the winter; $B_6$, zinc, and evening primrose oil for PMS and other menstrual problems—but high doses of single vitamins should not be taken without medical advice, because some of them can be toxic. Some vitamins also interfere with medication, so if you are taking prescribed medicines do check with your practitioner before starting to dose yourself.

Don't be fooled into thinking that it will not matter what you eat, as long as you take a vitamin pill. This simply is not true.

## VITAL VITAMINS

### VITAMIN A
➕ Essential for growth, skin, night- and color-vision.

➖ More than ten times the basic requirement of vitamin A, taken over long periods, can cause liver and bone damage. Do not take over 3,300μg during pregnancy, since there is a risk of causing birth defects.

GOOD SOURCES: liver, carrots, spinach, butter, margarine, broccoli, and Cheddar cheese.

### VITAMIN C
➕ Prevents scurvy, aids wound-healing and iron absorption, and is a vital and protective antioxidant.

➖ Do not take huge amounts of vitamin C without advice, as more than 1g per day has been known to cause diarrhea and to increase the risk of kidney stones in susceptible people.

GOOD SOURCES: blackcurrants, lemons, green bell peppers, oranges, grapefruit, kiwi fruit, and raw red cabbage.

### VITAMIN D
➕ Essential for bone formation, because it is part of the calcium absorption system.

➖ Ten times the daily requirement can be very toxic to children, and 25 times is dangerous for adults. Do not give more than one teaspoon of cod-liver oil to children each day, or exceed this during pregnancy.

GOOD SOURCES: cod-liver oil, oily fish, eggs, and margarine.

### VITAMIN B$_1$ (THIAMIN)
➕ Its main function occurs during the conversion of carbohydrates into energy.

GOOD SOURCES: cod roe, wheatgerm, brazil and peanuts, oatmeal, bacon, pork, organ meat, and bread.

### VITAMIN B$_2$ (RIBOFLAVIN)
➕ Vital for growth, and for the skin and mucous membranes.

GOOD SOURCES: eggs, milk, liver, kidneys, Cheddar cheese, beef, mackerel, almonds, cereals, and poultry.

### VITAMIN B$_6$ (PYRIDOXINE)
➕ Essential for growth, and many women find it can be helpful in treating PMS.

➖ Doses in excess of 2g a day can cause nerve damage and, in some particularly sensitive subjects, symptoms have occurred at intakes as low as 50mg.

GOOD SOURCES: fish, meat, liver, cheese, bananas, avocados, cod, salmon, and herring.

### FOLIC ACID
➕ Vital during growth and development; some birth defects may be related to a low intake of folic acid.

GOOD SOURCES: dark-green vegetables, liver, kidneys, nuts, wholewheat bread, and wholegrain cereals.

## MINERALS

There are certain minerals that your body needs—some in tiny amounts, others in intermediate amounts, and a few in minute traces. They are all essential, and missing out on any—even the trace minerals—can make the difference between health and sickness. These magic minerals are nearly always ignored when investigating health problems, except for iron and perhaps calcium. But the plain fact is that they are often a key factor in the cause of illness, and a simple supplement of the missing substances can produce dramatic improvements.

Two of the minerals, zinc and selenium, are of special interest to me, since they are the ones that can be used with dramatic effect, and which are often lacking in our diets. Zinc deficiency can be a factor in so many conditions, including anorexia nervosa and hyperactivity in children, while PMS and postnatal depression are just two conditions that almost always respond well to small doses of zinc; selenium deficiency can lead to low resistance, heart disease, skin problems, and a significantly increased risk of cancer, but you need to take only 100µg of selenium a day to make sure that your body never goes short of this vital element. Calcium is another magic mineral, of maximum importance during pregnancy, breastfeeding, childhood and teenage years, and to protect against osteoporosis in later years.

If your diet is a good, varied mixture of the main food groups, you

### RECOMMENDED DAILY ALLOWANCES

RDAs from the Food and Drug Administration

| Calcium | 1g |
|---|---|
| Iron | 18mg |
| Zinc | 15mg |
| Copper | 2.0mg |
| Sodium | 2,400mg |
| Potassium | 3,500mg |
| Magnesium | 400mg |
| Phosphorus | 1g |
| Iodine | 150µg |

µg = microgram

There are other minerals that play an important role in the way our bodies work, but for which there are not yet set RDAs, although maximum safe intake levels have been established.

are unlikely to need mineral pills, unless you have a particular health problem. But there are certain situations when a supplement is indicated, so here is my selection of the best combination of quality and value for money: selenium with vitamins A, C, and E; calcium with magnesium, boron, and vitamin D; zinc with vitamin C; zinc with copper, for long-term use; iron as amino acid chelate. A mineral complex is best when combined with amino acids to make it more easily available for the body to use.

*Read the labels carefully.* Some products do not supply very much of the minerals you actually need.

## MAGIC MINERALS

### ZINC

➕ Vital for growth, healthy sex organs, reproduction, insulin production, and for natural resistance.

➖ Too much zinc reduces the amount of copper in the body.

GOOD SOURCES: lamb, liver, steak, garlic, ginger root, brazil nuts, pumpkin seeds, oysters, eggs, sardines, oats, crab, almonds, and chicken.

### SELENIUM

➕ Part of the self-defense system and also important for cholesterol control and protection against some forms of cancer.

GOOD SOURCES: wholewheat bread made from North American flour, brazil nuts, butter, oily fish, liver, and kidneys.

### IRON

➕ Combines with oxygen to make hemoglobin, the red coloring of the blood, and transport oxygen to every cell of the body.

➖ Too much iron can lower your natural resistance and cause insomnia, tiredness, and depression.

GOOD SOURCES: edible seaweed, oily fish, shellfish, molasses, pig's liver, beef, pilchards, kidney beans, brazil nuts, dates, raisins, lentils, peanuts, chicken, soybeans, chick-peas, and peas.

### COPPER

➕ Works with iron to make red blood corpuscles.

GOOD SOURCES: oysters, nuts, beef, liver, lamb, butter, barley, olive oil.

### CALCIUM

➕ A vital mineral for the formation and continuing strength of bones, of maximum importance during pregnancy, breastfeeding, childhood and teenage years, and to prevent osteoporosis.

GOOD SOURCES: milk, yogurt, low-fat cheese, sardines (with the bones), green vegetables, dried fruit, nuts, beans, wholewheat bread, watercress, and parsley.

### IODINE

➕ Essential for the proper functioning of the thyroid gland.

➖ Too much iodine may cause overactivity of the thyroid; beware of taking too much of the kelp supplements.

GOOD SOURCES: edible seaweed, fish, and seafood.

### MANGANESE

➕ Needed for the formation of enzymes, bones, muscle action, and fertility.

GOOD SOURCES: wholegrain cereals, nuts, and tea.

### PHOSPHORUS

➕ Vital for bone formation, and as a constituent of cells.

GOOD SOURCES: foods that are rich in calcium.

### POTASSIUM

➕ Essential for the proper functioning of all the body's cells and nervous tissue.

GOOD SOURCES: bananas, oranges, avocados, nuts, legumes, dried fruit, potatoes, tomatoes, wholegrains.

## TOP 20 FOODS

The food entries throughout the book have shown which foods may help which systems of the body. This chart selects 20 of the most versatile foods and illustrates just some of the common ailments that they may help to benefit. For instance, bananas may be beneficial for childhood diseases, circulatory problems, constipation, diarrhea, fatigue, fluid retention, gastroenteritis, heartburn, infertility, insomnia, menstrual problems, nausea, PMS, and thrush.

| | Anemia | Arthritis | Asthma | Back pain | Catarrh | Childhood diseases | Circulatory problems | Colds | Constipation | Coughs | Cystitis | Diabetes | Diarrhea | Eczema | Fatigue | Fluid retention |
|---|---|---|---|---|---|---|---|---|---|---|---|---|---|---|---|---|
| Bananas | | | | | | ● | ● | | ● | | | | ● | | ● | ● |
| Brazil nuts | | | | | | ● | | | | | | | | | | |
| Cabbage | ● | ● | | ● | ● | ● | | | | | | | | | | |
| Carrots | | ● | | | ● | ● | | | | | | | ● | | | |
| Celery | | ● | | ● | | | | | | | ● | | | | ● | |
| Dates | ● | | | | | | | | ● | | | | | | ● | |
| Garlic | | | ● | | ● | ● | ● | ● | | ● | | | ● | | | |
| Ginger | | | | ● | | | | ● | | ● | | | | | | |
| Kiwi fruit | | | ● | | | ● | | | ● | | | | | | | |
| Lemons | | | | | ● | ● | ● | ● | | ● | | | | | | |
| Oats | | | | | | ● | ● | | ● | | | ● | | | | |
| Oily fish | | ● | | ● | | | | | | | | | | ● | | |
| Onions | | ● | ● | | ● | ● | ● | | | ● | | | | | | |
| Parsley | | | | ● | | | | | | | ● | | | | | ● |
| Pumpkin seeds | | | | | | ● | | | | | | | | ● | | |
| Soybeans | | | | | | | | | | | | | | | | |
| Spinach | ● | | | ● | | ● | | | | | | | | | | |
| Water | | | | | | ● | | ● | ● | | | | ● | ● | | ● |
| Wholewheat bread | | | | | | ● | | | ● | | | ● | | | | |
| Yogurt | | | | | | | | | | | ● | | ● | | | |

| | Gastroenteritis | Hay fever | Headaches | Heartburn | Indigestion | Infection | Infertility | Insomnia | Kidney problems | Menstrual problems | Nausea | Osteoporosis | PMS | Prostate problems | Rheumatism | Sinusitis | Sore throat | Thrush | Tonsillitis | Varicose veins |
|---|---|---|---|---|---|---|---|---|---|---|---|---|---|---|---|---|---|---|---|---|
| | • | | | • | | • | • | | | • | • | | | • | | | | • | | |
| | | | | | | | | | • | • | | | | • | | | | | | |
| | | | | | | | | | | | | | | | | | | | | |
| | | | | | | • | • | | | | | | | | | • | | | | • |
| | | | | | | | • | | | | | | | | • | • | | | | |
| | | | | | | | | | | | | | | | | | | • | | |
| | | • | | • | • | | | | | | | | | | | • | • | • | | |
| | | • | • | | | | | | | | • | | | | | | | | | |
| | | | | | | | | | | | | | | | | | | | | |
| | | • | | | | • | • | | | | | • | | | | • | • | | • | • |
| | | | | | | | • | • | | | • | | | | | | | • | | |
| | | | • | | | • | • | | | • | | | • | | • | | | • | | |
| | | • | | • | | | | | | | | | | | | | | • | | |
| | | | | | | | | • | | | | | • | • | | • | | | | |
| | | | | | | • | | | | | | | • | • | | | | • | | |
| | | | | | | • | | | | • | • | | | | | | | | | |
| | | | | | | • | | | | | | | | | | • | | | | |
| | • | | | | | | | | | • | | | | | | | | | • | |
| | | | | • | | | • | • | • | | | • | | | | | | | • | • |
| | | • | | | | | | | | | | • | | | | | | • | | |